STORIES *from* PERTH AMBOY

STORIES *from* PERTH AMBOY

KATHERINE MASSOPUST

Charleston · London

THE History PRESS

Published by The History Press
Charleston, SC 29403
www.historypress.net

Front cover: Courtesy of the Perth Amboy Free Public Library.
Back cover, top: Courtesy of the Massopust family; *bottom*: courtesy of Chester Freid.

First published 2012

Manufactured in the United States

ISBN 978.1.60949.696.8

Library of Congress CIP data applied for.

CONTENTS

CONTENTS

ACKNOWLEDGEMENTS

Stories from Perth Amboy came from an idea during a discussion with my mother, Marcella Massopust. I just started writing an outline, and more ideas came with it.

First, I would like to thank my husband, Paul W. Wang, for being there. I would like to extend my thanks to everyone who provided photos for this book: Donna Ross, Bob Ned, Chester Freid, Barbara Booz, Jack M. Dudas, Esq., Stephen Michael Dudash, Dr. Ryan Varga, D.C., Eleanor Bates, Paul W. Wang, the Proprietary House Historical Society, the Kearny Cottage Historical Society and the Perth Amboy Free Public Library.

I would like to thank Filomena Gianfrancesco for proofreading and Jack M. Dudas, Esq., for his input, suggestions and additional proofreading. I would also like to thank the Perth Amboy Historical Commission for its support.

For their interviews and comments, I would like to thank Arthur Brown, Daniel Yovanovich, Jack M. Dudas, Esq., Barbara Stack, Anne Rothlein, Eleanor Kataryniak, Carolyn Maxwell, Faith Hernandez, Bob Thullesen, Richard Hmieleski, Reggie Navarro, Marge Miller, Alma Cap and Ila Miller.

Acknowledgements

For help with research, thank you to the staff of Perth Amboy Free Public Library: Patricia Gandy, Herschel Chomsky, Edwin Olivarria, Manuel Sanpof, William Baez, Jessica Zulin and Vilma Novak.

I also want to thank my aunt, Joan Zaleski; my mother, Marcella Massopust; and my father, Perth Amboy city historian Anton J. Massopust, for their input, interviews and support.

INTRODUCTION

Upon our view and survey of the Ambo Point, we find it extraordinary, well situate for a great town or city, beyond expectation.[1]
—*Thomas Rudyard, first deputy royal governor, May 30, 1683*

Known as the City by the Bay, Perth Amboy is far from ordinary. It was described by one individual "as historic as it comes" and "on the top ten list of historic sites in America." Filled with rich and exciting history, there were many "firsts" in Perth Amboy. The first African American voter under the Fifteenth Amendment to the U.S. Constitution, Thomas Mundy Peterson, voted in the city hall of Perth Amboy. The Bill of Rights was first signed in Perth Amboy. The first flight of a dirigible took place in Perth Amboy. The list is quite extensive for this unique city.

For this book, I compiled sixteen stories about the town. These stories need to be told. After writing *Then and Now: Perth Amboy*, published by Arcadia with my husband, Paul W. Wang, I had a long talk with my mother, Marcella Massopust, and we started discussing how no one ever really made a concise and easily understandable documentation of Perth Amboy's history. Yes, you have the scholarly McGinnis and Whitehead, but I wanted to keep it interesting. The first chapter written was the KKK chapter. The rest of the book followed suit. Each story or vignette represents a story of a person, place or event in Perth Amboy's history that helped to shape the town in some way. There are some happy stories, some sad stories and some nostalgia.

Perth Amboy truly is a City of Great Expectation, and its potential is limitless.

Chapter 1

THE ARREST OF WILLIAM FRANKLIN

June 19, 1776

Although there is a great deal of speculation as to when William Franklin was born, according to his biographer, Shelia L. Skemp, Franklin was born sometime between September 1730 and March 1731 in the province of Pennsylvania.[2] However, most historians believe he was born in 1729 or 1730.[3] He is believed to be the illegitimate son of Benjamin Franklin and a woman whose name is lost to history, but historians speculate she was of the lower dregs of society. Neither William nor his father denied his illegitimacy, and the Franklins' enemies used it against them. Affectionately known as Billy, William grew up in high society. He was raised by Benjamin and his wife, Deborah Read Franklin, William's stepmother. Benjamin and Deborah had been married on September 1, 1730. Deborah's relationship with William was estranged from the start. She regarded William with "a coldness bordering on hostility."[4] Deborah and Benjamin would later have a son, Francis Folger Franklin (1732–1736). Lovingly known to the Franklins as Franky, he would die of smallpox at age four. On September 11, 1743, they would have a daughter, Sarah, who was fondly called Sally.

William grew up on lower Market Street in his father's print shop in the heart of Philadelphia. Benjamin Franklin believed in the philosophy of John Locke that children should be encouraged, nurtured and guided.

Benjamin Franklin, father of William Franklin and American Patriot. Benjamin Franklin traveled on several occasions to Perth Amboy to visit William to plead for his son to join the Patriot cause.

Sarah "Sally" Franklin, daughter of Benjamin and Deborah Read Franklin and sister of William Franklin. Sally was an avid Patriot during the American Revolution.

"William enjoyed an especially close relationship with his father, who was his friend, companion, and partner in a multitude of public, and private endeavors."[5]

William did not like academics, so he entered the military at an early age. He earned the rank of captain, but at age nineteen, he returned home to Philadelphia, where he helped his father with his experiments and scientific endeavors. It was William who held the kite with the key on it during that famous experiment in which Benjamin Franklin discovered electricity. From 1754 to 1756, William acted as controller of the general post office. In June 1755, William was the clerk of the Provincial Assembly. He accompanied the troops sent under the command of Benjamin Franklin to the forts of Pennsylvania. In 1757, Benjamin Franklin was appointed colonial agent to London. William would accompany his father to Europe.

William studied law and began practicing in 1758. He traveled with his father to England, Scotland, Flanders and Holland. William was known as a man of society. One of Ben Franklin's friends, William Strahan, wrote to Deborah:

> *Your son…I really think one of the prettiest young gentleman I ever knew from America. He seems to me to have a solidity of judgment, not very often to be met with in one of his years. This, with the daily opportunity he has of improving himself in the company of his father, who at the same time his friend, his brother, his intimate and easy companion, affords an agreeable prospect, that your husband's virtues and usefulness to his country may be prolonged beyond the date of his own life.*[6]

In 1762, Oxford University gave Benjamin Franklin an honorary degree in the doctor of laws for his proficiency in the natural sciences. William was also honored with an honorary master of arts degree for distinguishing himself at Oxford University. In August 1762, after undergoing a rigorous examination by Lord Halifax, minister of American affairs, and through the influence of Lord Bute—and not through any influence whatsoever from Benjamin—William was appointed the royal governor of New Jersey.

On September 4, 1762, at age thirty, William married Elizabeth Downes in a church in Hanover Square. In the future, William would have only one child, an illegitimate son, William Temple Franklin.[7] A week after he married Elizabeth, William took his oath as governor: "Bending his right knee, he took the king's hands into his own white gloved hands and kissed them, then rose to receive his commission and recite his oath of office."[8] William was proud of his new position, and so was his father—for the time being.

At that time there were two capitals of New Jersey: Burlington, the western capital, and Perth Amboy, the eastern capital. William at first chose to reside in Burlington, which helped him gain popularity among the local Quakers and other immigrants. William Franklin was welcomed by ringing church bells as he rode into Burlington. His father proudly rode by his side.

Franklin was considered a governor who "at times, indeed he sacrificed his own official popularity to the claims of personal friendship, and apprehensions of personal safety, or of prejudice to his interests, to

William Franklin, the son of Benjamin Franklin and the last royal governor of New Jersey. *Courtesy of the Proprietary House Organization.*

interfere with their adaptation in practice to the promotion of public welfare understood by him."[9] He was considered an able politician and a competent leader. "As governor, William Franklin encouraged legislation relating to the improvement of roads, the fostering of agriculture by the bestowment of bounties, and the melioration of the laws prescribing imprisonment for debt."[10] In 1766, he granted Queens College (now Rutgers University) its charter.

After years of serving as royal governor of New Jersey, William wanted a better job, but it was not meant to be. "He deeply resented the fact that in all those years of service, even as prices doubled and tripled he had received only one raise from the assembly. He was the lowest paid royal governor."[11] William blamed his father for his woes. Benjamin had a long-running feud with William's immediate superior, the colonial secretary. Any hope for being promoted was dismal in the least.

Elizabeth preferred London fashions and high society, as did William. "She decorated her sycamore-shaded townhouse in brilliant Georgian crimsons, golds, pale yellows. She imported an English maid to supervise the servants, even her husband instructed his coachman in the planting of elaborate formal gardens. When provincial politicians conversed each spring; Elizabeth entertained leaders and wives lavishly."[12] William was a man of fine tastes. In one letter to Benjamin, he requested his father order twenty custom-made mahogany side chairs for his parlor in Franklin Park.[13] Benjamin would unsympathetically ask for money that he claimed his son owed him. William would state that Benjamin kept poor records of what debts were paid and what debts were not paid.

Because William and Elizabeth could not afford their high-priced lifestyle, they decided it was cheaper to rent than own their own house. They decided to move into the Proprietary House in Perth Amboy in October 1774. He would move into the house "only after demanding that the Board paper the rooms, replace 176 broken window panes, build a stable and coach house and make other various expensive improvements."[14]

The Proprietary House was designed and constructed by John Edward Pryor, master builder. It was built by the proprietors of East New Jersey in 1762–64. The first occupant was Chief Justice Frederick Smythe, who lived there from 1766 to 1772. It was decided that the Proprietary House would be the home of the royal governor.

The Proprietary House, constructed 1762–64 by the East Proprietors of New Jersey and first occupied by Chief Justice Smythe. William and Elizabeth Franklin moved into the royal governor's mansion in October 1774. *Photo by the author.*

However, times were changing. The British government had begun to impose harsh measures on the people of the American colonies, including the infamous Stamp Act (1765), which stated that many printed materials in the colonies must be produced on stamped paper produced in London and carrying an embossed revenue stamp. These printed materials included legal documents, magazines, newspapers and many other types of paper. Like taxes imposed before by England, the stamp tax had to be paid in valid British currency, not in colonial paper money. It met with a great deal of opposition from the American colonies. Increasing numbers of the American populace opposed these harsh measures against the colonies, and they rapidly became disillusioned with British rule.

It was postwar (French and Indian War) America, and unemployment was rising. Many families had little money, and some had little food, rendering a situation conducive to rioting. The Stamp Act did not help the matter. Relations with England were becoming more and more estranged, and the insurgent movement grew. Benjamin Franklin was one of many Patriots who grew disenchanted with British rule of the colonies. "Benjamin Franklin had such a tendency toward vendetta that he sometimes lost all objectivity. His hatred for British aristocrats, as much as any set of deeply held principles, led him more and more to blame England for all the colonies grievances."[15]

On October 6, 1773, Benjamin wrote a letter to William stating that he should rethink his loyalty to England. It was the first of many letters that would urge William to renounce the king:

> *From a long and thorough consideration of the subject I am, indeed, of a opinion that the Parliament has no right to make any law whatever biding on the Colonies. That the King and not the King, Lords and Commons collectively, is their sovereign; and that the King, with their respective parliaments, is their only legislator. I know your sentiments differ from mine on these subjects. You are a thorough government man, which I do not wonder at, nor do I aim at converting you; I only wish you to act uprightly and steadily, avoiding that duplicity which in Hutchinson adds contempt to indignation. If you can promote the prosperity of your people, and leave them happier than you found them whatever your political principles are your memory will be honored.[16]*

Father and son would be divided over political views. In early November 1775, William welcomed his father's coach at the Proprietary House in Perth Amboy. He proudly gave Benjamin and his father's sister, Jane, a tour of the house. Jane had fled Boston under British rule, and they were making their way to Philadelphia. Benjamin made one last attempt in person to persuade William to renounce his loyalty to the King. Although it was for a brief visit, it would be the last time William would see his father until after the Revolutionary War. By the end of 1775, William and Ben had stopped corresponding, but the governor still did care for the man who had offered him so much guidance in his life. William would write to his son, William Temple Franklin, and inquire about Benjamin in every letter.

On January 2, 1776, the Continental Congress issued orders stating that all "unworthy Americans" be disarmed and, if necessary, imprisoned or forced to give word that they would do nothing to usurp the Patriot government. Cortlandt Skinner, a staunch supporter of Governor Franklin, had been cited as a Tory and fled the colonies in a rowboat escaping to a British man-of-war, leaving behind a wife and thirteen children.

Concern grew among the Patriots that Governor William Franklin was considered to be an enemy of the insurgence. Fear arose that William would flee just as Skinner had, although there was no proof that the governor was going anywhere. William Alexander, known as Colonel the Earl of Stirling or Colonel Stirling, felt that William Franklin needed to be apprehended, so he sent his right-hand man, Lieutenant William Winds, and ordered him to march to the eastern capital to arrest the royal governor.

At two o'clock in the morning, William and Elizabeth were awoken by "a violent knocking" at the front door. Elizabeth was so alarmed that William thought she might die of fright. He looked out the windows to see Continental soldiers surrounding the house. His greatest fear of being paraded around the country like a bear would come true. One of the servants opened the doors finally, and the man handed William a note from Colonel Winds stating he wanted a promise from William that he would not try to flee the country. "I have not the lest Intention to quit the Province," William stated proudly. "Nor shall I be compelled by Violence. Were I to act otherwise it would not be consistent with my Declarations to the Assembly, nor my regard for the good People of the Province." He handed his reply to the waiting servant.[17]

The soldiers remained, although Colonel Winds apologized for rousing the Franklins at such an early hour. William demanded to know by what authority he dared detain the King's servant. "You will," he warned Winds, "answer the contrary to your peril." By placing an officer of the King's government under house arrest, he had committed treason. And the penalty for treason was death.[18]

Winds felt awkward for William Franklin. William Franklin was the son of one of the Patriots' most regarded delegates and a royal governor and servant to the King. What to do with such a man was questionable, to say the least. The answer came on January 10, 1776, when Lord Stirling forwarded the exchange between Winds and Franklin to Philadelphia, insisting that William Franklin would not be silenced by house arrest. Following orders, about one hundred soldiers and a handful of officers rode to Perth Amboy to the Proprietary House. At first they "invited him to dinner with Lord Stirling." William did not fall for it, but he soon realized that he would be taken by force if necessary, so he started packing his bags. Just as the governor was going to surrender, Chief Justice Frederick Smythe galloped up to the Proprietary House. He was alarmed at the news that Franklin was about to be taken prisoner. Smythe had already dispatched a letter to Colonel Winds asking him to rescind his orders. Winds had promised to consider the request. Smythe rode frantically looking for Colonel Winds. The officers and men were restless and wished to depart for the city of Elizabeth before nightfall. William climbed into the coach with Stephen Skinner, who promised to be a character witness for William. They went three hundred yards when Smythe returned with one of Winds's officers with him. The colonel agreed to allow William to remain at the Proprietary House until Smythe pleaded his case personally to Lord Stirling. Smythe got Stirling to remove the guards, and Stirling made no further attempt to bother Franklin.

The rest of the winter was uneventful, and William regretted the chief justice's intervention. The governor believed that the British would eventually win the war and the leaders of the insurgence would be punished by the King's government once the British troops gained the upper hand. Although he did feel adamant of his office, "You may force me, but you shall never frighten me out of the Province."[19]

On June 14, 1776, the Provincial Congress under Samuel Tucker pronounced a direct order to arrest William Franklin: "That, in the opinion of this Congress, the said William Franklin, Esquire, has discovered himself to be an enemy to the liberties of this country; and that measures ought to be immediately taken for securing the person of the said William Franklin, Esquire."[20]

On the morning of June 17, 1776, Colonel Nathan Heard of Woodbridge, accompanied by Major Jonathon Deare of Perth Amboy, knocked on the door of the Proprietary House and handed William Franklin a parole to sign. Their orders: if the royal governor did not cooperate, they had no choice but to place him under arrest. William read the parole carefully and demanded to know by whose authority it was sent. Colonel Heard, prepared for such an answer, proceeded to hand Franklin two documents from New Jersey's Provincial Congress. William was amazed. As the Woodbridge militia surrounded the mansion, William went to his library and wrote frantically. Franklin defended himself, acting both as a lawyer and a politician, but he still refused to sign the parole. No one was allowed to visit the Proprietary House that night. Even Mrs. Franklin's doctor was turned away. Servants were followed by guards everywhere they went.

On June 19, William Franklin was arrested under the order of Colonel Nathan Heard of Woodbridge and Major Jonathan Deare of Perth Amboy with sixteen men armed with guns and bayonets. This time, William had no choice. He affectionately left his wife, Elizabeth, never to see her again. He was escorted to Burlington under close guard. It was now an object of mockery to be the royal governor, and William was humiliated. He was later taken and quartered in the house of Captain Ebenezer Grant of East Windsor. In 1778, William Franklin was exchanged along with the British royal governor of Delaware, John McKinley. William went back to New York City to find out that his wife had died, so he remained there for four years, the companion of James Rivington and other Loyalists. On August 13, 1782, he sailed for England. It was now twenty years after the King had appointed him royal governor of New Jersey. He was fed up with America.

Benjamin and William would meet for the last time in August 1785 on the French coast before Benjamin stopped in London and then returned to America. The meeting was a brief encounter and involved tying up outstanding legal matters. On August 14, 1788, William married Mary Johnson d'Evelin.

"During the years between the Revolution and the War of 1812 William lived a clubman's life in London. He was called 'The General' by his friends."[21] He often apologized for his relationship with Benjamin Franklin. He was featured in an article in *Public Characters* magazine, where he was cited as being a martyr to his principles and an honor to England. He lived the remainder of his life in England and died there on November 17, 1813, at age eighty-two.

Benjamin Franklin died on April 17, 1790 (age eighty-four), in Philadelphia, Pennsylvania. He left very little of his wealth to William (some land in Nova Scotia), stating that he would have nothing if the British had won the war. Deborah Read Franklin had died on December 24, 1774, when Benjamin was away in England. She had suffered a series of crippling strokes, the final one proving to be fatal. Elizabeth Franklin had been exiled to New York City, never to see her husband again. She died on July 25, 1778. Her remains are deposited in the Chancel of Trinity Episcopal Church in New York City. Ten years later, William had a tablet erected in her memory, which still to this day is present on the wall of St. Paul's Chapel of Trinity Church. William Temple Franklin resided in France, the companion of his grandfather, Benjamin, and the apple of his eye. William Temple Franklin was chosen to be the secretary to the American delegation at the Treaty of Paris in 1782–83, largely due to the influence of Benjamin. William Temple later became the biographer of Benjamin Franklin. He would have an illegitimate child, Ellen, born on May 15, 1798. William Temple died in Paris on May 25, 1823, ten years after his father passed away. Ellen Franklin died in Nice, France, in 1875, childless. William's sister, Sarah Franklin, would marry Richard Bache (1737–1811) on October 29, 1767, and have eight children. Sarah was an avid Patriot during the Revolutionary War. She helped to raise money for the Continental army and assisted in the sewing of clothing for the Patriots during the harsh winter at Valley Forge. She is known for her

Local performer Kurt Epps often portrays William Franklin at events such as the reenactment of the arrest of William Franklin. *Photo by the author.*

involvement with the Ladies Association of Philadelphia. She died on October 5, 1808, in Philadelphia at age sixty-five.

The arrest of William Franklin has been reenacted every year in June at the Proprietary House in Perth Amboy since the bicentennial in 1976. Local actor and performer Kurt Epps portrays the royal governor at the Arrest and at other local events as well.

Chapter 2

ELIZABETH LAWRENCE KEARNY

Madame Scribblerus
1751–1802

Elizabeth Lawrence was born in November 1751 in Perth Amboy. She was the daughter of Judge John Brown Lawrence and Ann Alice Leonard. A Quaker, Elizabeth was baptized on August 28, 1754, at St. Mary's Church in Burlington, New Jersey, by the Reverend Jonathan Odell. During her youth, she spent several winters in Philadelphia. Elizabeth was taught to speak fluent French as a child. Her excellent education and culture were encouraged by her parents.

The Lawrences were directly descended from Sir Robert Lawrence of Ashton Hall, Lancaster, England. During the twelfth century, Sir Robert Lawrence accompanied King Richard I to the Crusades in the Holy Land. For his services at Acre, Arsuf and Jaffa, he was knighted and received a coat of arms.

John Brown Lawrence was married twice. His first wife, Ann Leonard, was the daughter of Samuel Leonard, Esq., of Perth Amboy. They had one child, Elizabeth Lawrence. After her mother died, the young Elizabeth Lawrence was left in the care of her aunt, Rachel Leonard Sarjant. John Brown Lawrence then married Martha Tallman of Trenton. They would have seven children, five girls and two boys. Of the children, James Lawrence was the youngest. Elizabeth was fifteen years James's senior. Martha Tallman died when James Lawrence was an infant. A staunch Loyalist, John Brown Lawrence fled to Canada during the American Revolution, so Elizabeth was left to care for the infant, James. It is said of the early years when they lived in Burlington during the American Revolution that British ships would fire upon their house from the river. When a cannonball actually struck the building, it was taken as a sign that one of the family would die at the hands of the British. This omen came into being when Captain James Lawrence met his tragic fate during a naval battle in the War of 1812.

Elizabeth married Michael Kearny on June 30, 1774, at the age of twenty-two. Michael Kearny was the son of Philip Kearny and Isabella Hopper. Philip Kearny was the son of a Scotch-Irish immigrant, Michael Kearny, who came to live in Perth Amboy. Michael Kearny (Michael's grandson) was the son of a divided allegiance during the Revolutionary War but remained a Tory. During the war, he was held prisoner by the Provincial Congress of New Jersey. Upon his release, he served as a clerk in the British army and was made an officer in the voluntary militia of Loyalists. When the war ended, he accepted the new order, although his land had been confiscated.

Elizabeth Lawrence had inherited property from her grandfather, Captain Samuel Leonard, through her mother, Ann (Leonard) Lawrence. Michael Kearny built the Kearny Cottage on this property in 1781. The structure was originally located on High Street.

Michael and Elizabeth would have eight children, all boys: John, Robert, Michael, James,

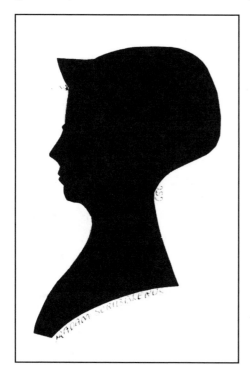

Known as "Madame Scribblerus" or "Pinderina," Elizabeth Kearny was famous for her poetry and writing for *Time Piece*, a tri-weekly literary journal. She was the half sister of Captain James Lawrence. *Courtesy of the Kearny Cottage Historical Society.*

Philip, Francis, William and Lawrence. The youngest was Commodore Lawrence Kearny, who was born and died in the Kearny Cottage. In total, five generations of Kearnys would live in the cottage. Each male of direct descent would serve as a vestryman in St. Peter's Episcopal Church.

Elizabeth was a noted writer of poetry and was given the name "Madame Scribblerus." She taught her half brother, Captain James Lawrence, the love of poetry. Elizabeth, under her pen name, wrote of her brother James:

> *My brave, brave Jim's a sailor Jack*
> *Upon the treacherous sea—*
> *A sailor who loves poetry*
> *All taught to him by me.*[22]

During the War of 1812, Captain James Lawrence had taken command of the frigate USS *Chesapeake*. He left port in Boston Harbor on June 1, 1813, and immediately engaged the blockading Royal Navy frigate HMS *Shannon* in a fierce battle. The British ship disabled the *Chesapeake*

Half brother of Elizabeth Lawrence, Captain James Lawrence of the USS *Chesapeake* was famous for saying, "Don't give up the ship!"

with gunfire within the first few minutes. Captain Lawrence, mortally wounded by small arms fire, ordered his officers with an unconquerable spirit: "Don't give up the ship. Fight her 'til she sinks! Or tell them to fire faster; don't give up the ship!" His crew carried him below, but his men were overwhelmed by a British boarding party shortly afterward. James Lawrence died of his wounds three days later on June 4, 1813.

After James Lawrence's death, the story of his passing was reported to his friend and fellow officer Oliver Hazard Perry. Perry ordered a large blue battle ensign stitched with the phrase "DON'T GIVE UP THE SHIP" in bold white letters. The Perry flag would be flown on his flagship during a victorious naval battle against the British on Lake Erie in September 1813.

To Perth Amboy and the literary world of her day, Elizabeth Lawrence Kearny was better known by her pen names, "Madame Scribblerus" or "Pinderina," which reflected the romantic fashion of the day. Her intimate friends included the most prominent people of culture in the early days of the United States. In the first years of her marriage, she made two or three journeys to Philadelphia to visit old friends. "Among her personal friends were Peggy Chew, a noted Quaker City belle who replaced Honoara Sneyd in Major John Andre's affections; the famous Shippen sisters; and the dazzling Mrs. Bingham."[23] The Shippen sisters—Peggy, Sarah, Elizabeth and Mary—were daughters of a prominent family in Philadelphia. It was Peggy Shippen who had fallen in love with Major Andre but instead married Benedict Arnold and is believed to be the driving force behind Arnold's treason. "The dazzling Mrs. Bingham" was a name given by Abigail Adams to the beautiful and rich Ann Willing Bingham. Ann's husband derived his wealth through trade and land speculation. The couple liked the good life and indulged themselves, often to the point of excess. The Binghams had the city's most ostentatious mansion of the era constructed on Spruce Street in Philadelphia. Ann Bingham was also known for her risqué repartee. The Binghams were sought-after guests in the monarchial courts of Europe.

This piece shows Elizabeth's clever wit:

"Lines on Mrs. Bingham's Recall of a Supper Invitation"
Just in from the country, with nothing to wear,
At Bingham's tonight I am bidden repair.

My one silken pelisse is all in a tangle,
And I know I have lost my Parisian bangle.
Not a whiff of hair-powder to light up my head—
Methinks 'twould be better to get into bed!
My slippers the parrot has quite eaten up—
Oh! why am I bidden to come in to sup?
Now, Rebecca, do try to make that child stop its wailing;
At the thought of the company courage is failing!
There's a chair going past and coach with a clatter.
If I go as I am—pray, what does it matter?
Here give me some Rose-Bloom to ease up my face,
And a patch on my chin would give it a grace.
My new brilliant necklace, my white turkey wrapping;
Ah, now I am ready; but who is that tapping?
A word from the Binghams—you say a postponement:
An illness—alas 'tis a hurried atonement,
With nothing to wear, and nothing to eat!
Come blow out the candles and gaze on the street.
Madame Scribblerus[24]

Some people—such as Betsy Parker of the famous Parker Castle in Perth Amboy—were not pleased with Elizabeth's writings. In a letter to her sister Janet, Betsy wrote, "Oh why won't Madame Scribblerus stop her scribbling?"[25]

Despite her critics, Elizabeth Kearny had many enthusiasts. One ardent admirer wrote of Elizabeth Kearny, "She occupies the highest seat on Parnassus."[26] Parnassus is a mountain of limestone in central Greece that towers above Delphi.

Madame Scribblerus was a frequent contributor to *Time Piece*, a tri-weekly literary journal conducted by Philip Freneau in New York. *Time Piece* was a rival of the *Porcupine Gazette*, a highly praised journal edited by William Cobbet. During the time he was in charge of *Time Piece*, Freneau had many female literary hopefuls corresponding with him. Elizabeth Kearny was by far his largest contributor. She also visited Freneau in his Monmouth home, Mount Pleasant Hall. Elizabeth also published in local newspapers and circulated her poetry among her friends.

One piece of poetry she wrote was to a couple:

"To the Pennington's on Their Marriage"
May you like Isaac and Rebecca live,
And each receive happiness you give,
No clouds arrive make your prospects dark,
No winds tempestuous, adverse toss your barque,
No slander by the fiend-like envy led,
O'er you, my friends, her sooty pinions spread,
Nor Jealousy, (the Lover's Hell) e'er find.
You to her baleful whisperings inclin'd
But may you smoothly pass the stream of life,
One a fond Husband, One a loving Wife;
And when you go to your great reward to claim
Your children heir your fortune and your fame.
Madame Scribblerus[27]

We can picture to ourselves Elizabeth working away with her goose quill pen in the Kearny Cottage far into the night, with only a primitive candle to her labors.

Many and many a tired reveler, leaving those famous Brighton House balls in their heyday at the Old Franklin Palace long before 1812 brought gloom and war, must have stopped before the light casting its glow from her chamber window and been cheered by the thought that someone was awake as he faced the darkness of old Amboy lanes and alleys.[28]

The blue-stockinged Pinderina lost her taste for grand social events such as the Brighton House balls. She was often far more proper than society demanded at the time. Since Michael had died in 1791, Elizabeth had no desire to attend such elaborate affairs, which were so common at the time in Perth Amboy, and wished to keep mainly to herself. During the anniversary of his death, Elizabeth compiled two or three hundred verses of poetry dedicated to "her beloved Michael's" memory, demonstrating the love she had for her husband.

The seventh volume of her unpublished poetry still survives. During the last years of the eighteenth century, the United States came upon unpleasant terms with France. Elizabeth herself began despising France, calling the French "frog-eaters." It was during the beginning of Thomas Jefferson's administration that Madame Scribblerus, interested in the sentiments of Perth Amboy, which at the time was an important New Jersey seaport, voiced her opinion in:

"An Epigram"
Say William to Thomas I'll hold you a bet
That the French are Confoundedly frightened;
They thought they Federal Ships had o'ereset;
But they find that they staunch are, and righted.
They slighted our Pleno's and made a demand
That we shameful Tribute should pay them,
Or else (as they plundered at Sea) on the Land
Neither Rapine nor Murder shall stay them!
But those who are born in the woods can't be scared
By the croaking of Bull-frogs in ditches.
Nor will we of Frenchmen at all be afraid,
A people who're sans honor, sans breeches.
They've taken our coats from our backs and say too
That they will have our shirts and smocks, sir;
But faith if they try it the project they'll rue
For we'll give them flesh burning knocks, sir!
They've tried ev'ry art which deception will frame,
But Our Congress too wise were to heed them.
They've Heaven defied, and put aside shame,
And have gone all lengths the Devil will lead them.
Madame Scribblerus[29]

Elizabeth died in 1802 in Perth Amboy and is buried in St. Peters Churchyard. Her grave is marked by a white, flat stone, which she shares with her husband, Michael, and child, William Kearny.

The Kearny Cottage is now owned by the City of Perth Amboy and maintained by the Kearny Cottage Historical Society. The building was moved from its former location on High Street in the 1930s to where the tennis courts are now and then to 63 Catalpa Avenue, where it remains today.

Elizabeth Lawrence was placed on the Women's Heritage Trail on Sunday, June 10, 2012. *Left to right*: Vilma Novak, reenactor Jeffrey Macechak as Captain James Lawrence, Katherine Massopust and Filomena Gianfrancesco. *Photo by Paul W. Wang.*

Elizabeth Kearny never expected much from her writing. In one poem she expressed:

> *If you think a reward is due for my Lays,*
> *Pray give me a small sprig of the Bays;*
> *But writings like mine I'm afraid do not claim*
> *One Leaf from a Tree which is sacred to fame.*[30]

But Elizabeth Kearny, aka Madame Scribblerus, aka Pinderina, was honored and remembered. She was placed on the Women's Heritage Trail at the Kearny Cottage on Sunday, June 10, 2012.

Chapter 3

AARON BURR STAYS AT THE TRUXTUN HOUSE

July 22, 1804

There is some speculation that this is a legend, and there is no proof that Aaron Burr actually came to Perth Amboy, but some historians believe he did.

A aron Burr is remembered as the man who shot and killed Vice President Alexander Hamilton, turned traitor and was a womanizer.[31] Aaron Burr was born in Newark, New Jersey, on February 6, 1756. His mother, Esther Burr, was the daughter of the famous Reverend Jonathon Edwards, the most influential theologian in America. Esther Burr was a spirited woman who was opinionated, religious without being stuffy and well educated. Aaron Burr's father, Aaron Burr Sr., had been a Presbyterian minister since 1736 and was president of the College of New Jersey. Aaron had a sister, Sally, who was two years older than him. By 1757, the family had moved to Princeton, New Jersey. Tragedy struck the Burr family in the years to come. Aaron Burr Sr. died of an illness on September 23, 1757, after a trip to Elizabethtown. Aaron Jr. would become ill as well, but he soon got well. Esther's father, Jonathon Edwards, moved to Princeton and died of smallpox in March 1758. Esther Burr then died on April 7, 1758. Sarah Edwards (Aaron's grandmother) came to take care of affairs, and she fell ill from dysentery and died on October 2, 1758. Aaron and Sally were now orphans. A family friend,

Aaron Burr, vice president of the United States under Thomas Jefferson from 1801 to 1804. Remembered as the man who shot Alexander Hamilton, Burr allegedly came to Perth Amboy after the infamous duel with Hamilton and stayed at the Truxtun House.

Dr. William Shiper of Philadelphia, took care of them for a while, but in 1760, two years after the death of their parents, Timothy Edwards, Esther's younger brother, took in the children. Timothy and his wife, Rhoda Ogden, took care of a brood that included five aunts and uncles (Esther's younger sisters and brothers ranging from ten to twenty years old); Rhoda's younger brothers Matthias and Aaron Ogden; and Aaron and Sally Burr. Timothy and Rhoda would also have fifteen children of their own.

Aaron grew up an avid scholar, although he ran away from home on several occasions. The family moved from Stockbridge, Massachusetts, to Elizabethtown, New Jersey. At that time, most boys followed in the profession that their father pursued. To do something different was unusual. Timothy Edwards hired Tapping Reeve, a Princeton graduate, to supervise Aaron and Sally's education. In 1769, at the age of thirteen, Aaron was accepted into Princeton (at the time a sort of prep school/college). His nickname was "Little Burr" because of his age. Aaron would study eighteen hours a day. He also joined clubs in Princeton: the Whig

Society and later the Cliosophic Society. "Far more than classrooms, clubs polished character, encouraged verbal contests, and created intense highly emotional fraternal bonds."[32]

Aaron Burr graduated in 1772 and entered the Continental army and fought with Benedict Arnold in Quebec. Burr escaped imminent danger and was commended for intrepid conduct. He was sent up the St. Lawrence River to reach General Richard Montgomery, who had taken Montreal, and escorted him to Quebec. Montgomery promoted Burr to captain and made him an aide-de-camp. Montgomery would die in the attempt to take Quebec. Burr was then assigned in Manhattan to General George Washington, who was said to take an immediate dislike to him. Burr quit after two weeks because he wanted to return to the battlefield. General Israel Putnam took Burr under his wing. By his vigilance in the retreat from lower Manhattan to Harlem, Burr saved an entire brigade (including Alexander Hamilton, who was one of its officers) from capture after the British landing on Manhattan. General Washington failed to commend Burr's actions in the next day's general orders (this was the fastest way to obtain a promotion in rank). Although Burr was already a nationally known hero, he never received a commendation. On June 27, 1777, Burr was promoted to lieutenant colonel in the Continental army and assigned to Colonel William Malcolm's regiment stationed at Smiths Clove Ramapo Mountains of New York State. On June 28, 1778, Burr would fight in the Battle of Monmouth and suffer heat stroke. He resigned from the Continental army in March 1779 because of health issues.

In September 1777, Burr met Theodosia Prevost, ten years his senior. She was married to a British officer and had five children. She also had a secret romance with Aaron Burr. Theodosia managed to openly be a Patriot and garner their support while at the same time convincing everyone that she was a Loyalist. She would spy for the Patriots and aid her circle of male patrons. Theodosia's husband passed away from yellow fever in Jamaica in December 1781. Theodosia then openly became lovers with Aaron Burr and encouraged him to become a lawyer. They were married on July 2, 1782, two months after he was approved as a lawyer. They had a daughter, Theodosia, born June 21, 1783, their only child to survive to adulthood.

They moved to New York City as Burr's practice thrived. "They both believed that intelligent women could participate in politics."[33] Not only did Burr advocate education for women, but upon his election to the New York State legislature, he submitted a bill to allow women to vote. Both Aaron and Theodosia the elder saw to it that Theodosia the younger was well educated with a rigorous curriculum. Burr was a slave owner and also made certain that his slaves were educated.

Theodosia the elder died in 1794 of stomach cancer. In January 1798, Burr was in the state capital of Albany and in the state assembly. He became an indispensible power broker. "As a leader of the assembly he shaped a progressive commercial agenda that promoted internal improvements, a fairer tax system, liberal banking practices, lower municipal taxes and debtor relief."[34] By the time he was voted out of office in 1799, he had turned the entire state from predominantly Federalist to Democrat-Republican, which alarmed his Federalist enemies.

Some of Burr's political moves did not work. He assisted the Dutch-owned Holland Land Company, which purchased 3.3 million acres of land in New York State. The company's owner, Theophile Cazenove, wanted a law passed allowing non-Americans to own land outright. At the time, it was typical for Americans to hold deeds for foreigners. In 1796, the law stated that if the land was not in American hands it went back to the state. Burr asked Alexander Hamilton for help. Through a deal, the Holland Land Company would get an extension to 1816 if it agreed to pay the Western Lock Navigation Company $250,000 (the president was Philip Schuyler, Hamilton's father-in-law) to keep its canal company afloat. The deal fell through, and Aaron Burr one year later helped to get a law passed to help Cazenove, the Alien Landowners Act. In the process to get it passed, Burr bribed Josiah Ogden, the New York attorney general; Thomas Morris, state senator; and a Mr. L. (anonymous). Burr then proceeded to buy a large tract of land from Cazenove in an attempt to make a profit. Burr consequently could not sell the land and had to return the 20,000 acres to the company.

Burr's next mistake was with the Manhattan Company, an attempt to provide fresh water to New York City and at the same time function as a bank. Alexander Hamilton joined him in his efforts in order to secure his brother-in-law John Bank Church a position in the company. The company had a clause in its charter that it could not be dissolved aside from government intervention. Burr was ousted from the board of directors in 1802. All these actions painted Burr as a "fanatic" or "radical" whose politics threatened to turn America into a colony of revolutionary France by overturning the existing social order.[35]

"At this time in American history, presidential races were most often decided in state legislatures—where the power to name electors resided."[36] When the election of 1800 came about, Burr used his military experience to name the electors and put together an unbeatable slate— one that would vote for him for president. The election of 1800 was controversial. It was the first peaceful transition of power from the ruling party (Federalist) to the opposing party (Democrat-Republican). The fact that Burr was willing to steal the election from Jefferson added to Burr's unpopularity. Thomas Jefferson would receive seventy-three electoral votes, Aaron Burr seventy-three and John Adams sixty-five, with the other votes divided among other candidates. The vote went to the House of Representatives, and John Adams went to it urging to make Thomas Jefferson president. Aaron Burr would then become vice president.

In 1800, Washington City became the nation's capital. Aaron Burr was popular with the military, which called him "Colonel Burr." Alexander Hamilton often had his hand in pamphlets blaspheming Burr. Aaron Burr was a threat to Alexander Hamilton's power, and Hamilton viewed it as his "religious duty to oppose his career."[37] When Burr ran for U.S. senator, Hamilton wrote private letters claiming, among other things, that "his integrity as an individual is not unimpeached…as a public man he is of the worst sort."[38] Hamilton also was a thorn in Burr's side; any time he ran for office, his character was always in question. "Alexander Hamilton's fear of Aaron Burr's ability to appeal to Federalists as well as Republicans stirred the General to rancorous—and extremely unchristian—slander."[39] Hamilton was certain evil would come of a Burr victory as vice president. He was sure it would lead to the secession of New York and the New England states, with Burr as their leader. He was equally pessimistic about the reckless assault on the judiciary in Washington, D.C., and in Pennsylvania. He lamented to Judge James Kent the "sway of artful and ambitious demagogues."[40] In 1801, the *American Citizen* published a letter written by James Cheetham comparing Aaron Burr to the Roman degenerate Catiline. Mayor DeWitt Clinton also verbally assaulted Burr. Burr's name was often slandered in the New York newspapers, and Burr blamed Hamilton when he heard of Hamilton's slanderous letters written about him. On April 24, 1804, the

Albany Register published a letter by Dr. Charles D. Cooper slandering Burr. When Burr found out of these slanderous accusations, he left New York to prove he was not a traitor to his party and determined to restore his honor. He demanded an apology from Alexander Hamilton, whom he was certain was behind the slander. Hamilton refused. "As General Hamilton—the one public role he still reserved for himself—he could not let Colonel Burr humiliate him. He had no doubt if he wrote a humble apology to Burr; it would appear in the *Morning Chronicle* the next day. That would almost certainly destroy whatever influence General Hamilton might still have in the New York Federalist Party."[41] He refused to apologize, so Burr challenged him to a duel.

Alexander Hamilton stated that he was morally opposed to dueling; nevertheless, he accepted the challenge. Dueling was illegal in New York, so they traveled to Weehawken, New Jersey, on July 11, 1804, for the fight. They tossed a coin to decide who would have choice of position and who would order the fire. Nathaniel Pendleton would be the one to order the

Alexander Hamilton, political rival of Aaron Burr, met his fate in the duel with Burr in Weehawken, New Jersey, on July 11, 1804. Hamilton would die from his wounds two days later.

fire. Hamilton was positioned with his back to the cliff and Burr his back to the glistening water. Church pistols were the weapon of choice, and powder and a "smooth ball" were used for ammunition. Technically, the barrels of the guns were smooth and the spinning bullet was not very accurate.

It was approaching seven o'clock. The duelists walked thirty yards. Pendleton yelled to ask if the two were ready. They were. He yelled, "Present!" and the men were free to fire their weapons. Burr's man, William P. Van Ness, thought that Hamilton fired first, and Hamilton's man, Pendleton, thought that Burr fired first. However, when the smoke cleared, it was evident that Hamilton was shot, mortally wounded. Burr had won the duel.

After the duel with Alexander Hamilton, Aaron Burr went to New York. He had fatally wounded Hamilton, who died two days later of his wounds. Burr's friends urged him to leave New York due to growing ill feelings about the duel. Burr argued that the duel was a fair fight and Hamilton had voluntarily taken part in it and lost. Ignoring warnings, Burr stayed in Richmond Hill, New York, for ten days until Saturday, July 21, when he finally boarded a barge at 10:00 p.m. that his friends provided for him and rowed down the Hudson shore near Richmond Hill and down the river. Burr decided that reason and evidence were not enough to save him from indictment for murder. Burr was accompanied by his friend Samuel Swartwout and Peter, his Negro servant. Swartwout was a close ally of Burr. They slept in the stern of the boat, and the men helping Burr rowed all night. They rowed through New York Harbor and around Staten Island to Perth Amboy, New Jersey.

By nine o'clock the next morning, Sunday, July 22, they were off to the Perth Amboy shore by "the Bluff" near Pleasant View, home to Commodore Thomas Truxtun. Truxtun was a retired naval officer, former commander of the USS *Constellation* and the USS *President*. He was noted for his victory over the French vessel *L'Insurgente* in the undeclared Quasi-War (1798–99). Truxtun was now retired and living in Perth Amboy. The old commodore was disgusted at how Thomas Jefferson had nearly dismantled the U.S. Navy and deplored Jefferson's administration. Burr sent Peter ashore to tell Commodore Truxtun that the vice president of the United States was on a boat offshore waiting to come ashore. Aaron Burr was not sure how the commodore would receive him.

It turned out that the commodore was sympathetic to Burr. He felt that under Code Duello, Burr was justified in challenging Hamilton to a duel. Commodore Truxtun hurried to see the barge starting to drift offshore. Truxtun welcomed Aaron Burr into his house as he made his landing. Truxtun gave Burr some coffee while Samuel Swartwout had breakfast and then immediately left back for New York. Little was said of the duel. Burr wished for safe passage to Cranbury, New Jersey, in order to go to Philadelphia. The next day, which was Monday, Truxtun granted his wish and escorted Aaron Burr with his own horse and carriage to Cranbury, where Burr took the Bristol ferry and then took the stage and

The Bluff, circa early 1900s. Many residents thought of the Bluff as the residential area of choice, where expensive Victorian homes lined both sides of the street. Many influential families had homes along the Bluff, and many residents of the Bluff had private beaches. During the early 1800s, Commodore Thomas Truxtun's home was also on the Bluff. *Courtesy of Dr. Ryan Varga, D.C.*

made his way to Philadelphia. Commodore Truxtun then wrote a long letter to the *New York Evening Post* defending himself and his actions and Aaron Burr's actions.

Burr was charged with murder in New York and New Jersey, but neither charge ever reached trial. Burr was actually indicted for murder in New Jersey in November 1804, even though dueling was legal in New Jersey, but the Supreme Court in Bergen County squashed the indictment on a motion from Colonel Ogden. Burr fled to South Carolina, where his daughter, Theodosia, lived with her family. He later returned to Washington, D.C., to complete his term of service as vice president. After he finished his term, Aaron Burr delivered a heartfelt farewell speech in March 1805 that would move some of his harshest critics in the Senate to tears.

Afterward, Burr went west, since his political career was considered over. He became involved in "filibuster plans," which some later claimed were intended to establish a new independent empire comprising land from the newly acquired Louisiana territory. Later, Burr conceived plans to emigrate and take possession of land in the Texas territories leased to him by the Spanish. However, General James Wilkinson, who had worked with Burr, backed out of their plans. Wilkinson then decided to betray Aaron Burr to President Jefferson and to his Spanish paymasters. Jefferson issued an order for Burr's arrest, declaring him a traitor even before any kind of indictment. Burr was charged with treason for assembling an armed force to take New Orleans and separate the western from the Atlantic states. He was also charged with high misdemeanor for sending a military expedition against territories belonging to Spain.

Burr's trial proved to be a major test of the Constitution. It was watched by the public with careful eyes. During the trial, it was revealed that Burr had a secret correspondence with Anthony Merry and the Marquis of Casa Yrujo, the British and Spanish ministers at Washington. In actuality, this correspondence had been for the purpose of securing money and to hide Burr's real plans, which were to help Mexico overthrow Spanish power in the Southwest and to found a dynasty in what would have become the former Mexican territory. Because of the laws at the time, these actions were viewed as a misdemeanor.

Jefferson sought the highest charges against Burr. It has been said that George Hay, the prosecuting U.S. attorney, compiled a list of more than 140 witnesses, including Andrew Jackson. Burr was arraigned a total of four times for treason before a grand jury finally indicted him. Despite an indictment, the government had a weak case; the only physical evidence actually presented to the grand jury was Wilkinson's so-called letter from Burr proposing stealing land in the Louisiana Purchase. During the jury's examination, it was discovered that the letter was in Wilkinson's own handwriting—a copy, he said, because he had lost the original. Consequently, the grand jury threw the letter out, and the newspapers ridiculed the general for the rest of the proceedings.

Article 3, Section 3 of the United States Constitution requires that treason either be admitted in open court or proved by an overt act witnessed by two people. Since no two witnesses came forward, Burr was finally acquitted. Afterward, he was tried on a misdemeanor charge but was again acquitted.

His wealth gone, Burr went to Europe in 1808 to try to make some sort of life for himself. In 1812, he returned to New York to resume his law practice. He died in Staten Island, New York, in the village of Port Richmond in 1836 at the age of eighty. He is buried in Princeton, New Jersey, near his father. Aaron Burr would never apologize to the Hamilton family for the duel.

Chapter 4

LAWRENCE KEARNY

The Sailor Diplomat
November 30, 1789–November 29, 1868

Born in Perth Amboy, New Jersey, on November 30, 1789, Lawrence
Kearny was the son of Michael Kearny and Elizabeth Lawrence.
Michael's grandfather Michael Kearny had emigrated from Cork,
Ireland, to New York in 1704 and then came to Perth Amboy around
1720. Michael Kearny (grandson) was born in Perth Amboy in 1751
and was twenty years old during the Revolutionary War. He was a
Tory, and in 1776, he was held prisoner by the Provincial Congress
of New Jersey. After his release, he went to New York and served as a
clerk for the British army. He later served as an officer in the voluntary
militia of Loyalists. Although his estate had been confiscated, Michael
returned to Perth Amboy after the war was over and married Elizabeth
Lawrence on June 30, 1774. Elizabeth inherited land from her
grandfather. On that land, Michael built the Kearny Cottage, which
stood on High Street.

Throughout the eighteenth century, the Kearnys had been a
prominent family in the area. Together, Michael and Elizabeth had eight
sons, two of whom were destined for greatness: Lawrence and Francis.
The youngest, Lawrence Kearny, was born in the cottage. The family
belonged to St. Peter's Episcopal Church, with each male in the line of
Kearnys serving as a vestryman.

Built in 1871 on High Street in Perth Amboy by Michael Kearny Jr., the Kearny Cottage was home to Lawrence Kearny, who was born and died in the cottage. When the last Kearny descendant passed away in the 1920s, a group of concerned citizens moved the cottage to the waterfront to preserve it. It is now a museum maintained by the Kearny Cottage Historical Society. *Courtesy of the Massopust family.*

Born in 1780, Francis Kearny became one of the most prominent engravers of his time. In New York, he was a member of the Tanner, Vallance, Kearny & Company firm, and then later in Philadelphia the firm became Pendleton, Kearny & Childs. Francis Kearny died in 1837. Lawrence Kearny enlisted in the U.S. Navy and was appointed midshipman on July 24, 1807. He entered the navy for several reasons:

> *Though his mother had died when he was still a boy, her strong nationalism continued to influence him. Furthermore, he could not escape the glamour cast by his uncle, the gallant and fascinating James Lawrence, who when Kearny was at the impressionable age of fifteen had taken a leading part under Stephen Decatur in the destruction of the captured* Philadelphia *in the harbor of Tripoli.*[42]

His first orders as midshipman in New York were to join gunboat *39* in the flotilla under John Rodgers. Kearny described his commander as "one of the best." The gunboats were called "The Jeffs" and were in all practicality a makeshift navy. They were low-cost boats that President Thomas Jefferson employed as naval defense in Long Island Sound, Chesapeake Bay and the sounds and inlets in the Carolinas and Georgia. The purposes of these vessels were to enforce the embargo and protect coasting trade.

After a short period, Kearny was assigned to the USS *Constitution* and the USS *President*, two of the finest frigates in the navy. These ships would cruise up and down the coast to protect American shipping. In the following year, Kearny was transferred to the USS *Enterprise* under the command of Lieutenant B.F. Reed. On its way to New Orleans, the ship ran into a heavy gale and was dismasted. It pulled into Norfolk for repairs, and Johnston Blakely was given command. Kearny served under him for two years and stated that Blakely was one of the keenest and most resourceful of the young officers of the time. Kearny was then in some important engagements in the War of 1812.

He received a commission as lieutenant on March 6, 1813, and commanded the schooners USS *Caroline*, USS *Ferret* and USS *Nonsuch* and later a flotilla of galleys and barges. In 1815, Kearny was given command of the USS *Enterprise*. "Piracy was now becoming increasingly common in southern waters and those about the West Indies, nor did the marauders limit their operations to the unfrequented shores. In September 1821, the schooner *Union* was plundered a little to the south of Cape Henry and the schooner *Evergreen* captured off Havana."[43] The reason for much of the preying upon local commerce was due to the unsettled conditions of Latin American countries that had recently freed themselves from Spanish rule. In 1821, Kearny captured pirates off southern Cuba.

On March 3, 1825, Lawrence Kearny was promoted to master commandant and given the USS *Warren* to command in the Mediterranean. There he convoyed American ships to Smyrna and patrolled the waters of the Cyclades. He captured seven boats belonging to pirates and recovered much stolen property. Kearny was so good at capturing pirates that the English critics stated that he did more with his little American flotilla than any other country. On December 27, 1832, Kearny was promoted to captain. Commodore Kearny was known for his tenacity in capturing slave traders in West Indian waters and his efforts in fighting Greek pirates in the Mediterranean Sea.

Known as "the sailor diplomat," Lawrence Kearny was famous for fighting pirates in the Mediterranean and Caribbean, opening up trade with China and freeing Hawaii from British rule. He was also mayor of Perth Amboy. *Courtesy of the Kearny Cottage Historical Society.*

In 1834, Lawrence Kearny married Josephine C. Hall, with the ceremony taking place in Trinity Episcopal Church in New York City. Kearny was forty-four and Josephine was eighteen. His new wife's two younger sisters, Ann Louisa and Mary E. Hall, were treated as though they were Kearny's own daughters, so they and their little brother, "Little Ned," came to live with them in the cottage in Perth Amboy. Kearny paid for their schooling and welcomed them with open arms. Lawrence and Josephine would have two sons: James Lawrence, born April 19, 1846, and John Michael, born November 6, 1848.

By 1839, China was suffering through the first Opium War, and British opium traders failed to distinguish between English-speaking people of European ancestry. In 1841, Commodore Kearny was given command of the forty-two-year-old frigate USS *Constellation* and the sloop USS *Boston* and sent to China. He arrived in Macau in March 1842, at the conclusion of the Opium War, and offered a treaty for trade. Kearny's orders were to protect the United States' interests, respect foreign and domestic policies of China and prevent and punish opium smuggling under the guise of the American flag. The Opium War had ended, and letters poured into China from American merchants demanding reparations for damages. Kearny was fair when addressing these claims. Viceroy Ke, in Guangzhou, wrote to the United States vice-consul: "I've heard that the newly arrived Commodore manages affairs with clear understanding, profound wisdom, and great justice." The viceroy committed China to abide by Kearny's decisions regarding the claims. As a result of Kearny's work, several hundred thousand dollars were paid to American merchants. A treaty was offered by Ke giving Americans fair treatment. Although Kearny did not have the authority to sign it, he stated that the United States would agree to the terms. This marked the beginning of the open-door trade policy in China. When Caleb Cushing arrived in China, the Treaty of Wanghia was signed on July 2, 1844. Lawrence Kearny laid the foundation for future relations with China for years to come. He had earned the nickname "the sailor diplomat." He accomplished what no one could do before.

When Kearny returned to the United States, he stopped off at Hawaii on his return voyage in July 1843 and learned that King Kamehameha III had surrendered the islands to Great Britain after being threatened by Lord Paulet. Kearny refused to recognize the British takeover until English, United States and Hawaiian representatives discussed the matter. Two weeks later, England's senior officer in the Pacific, Rear Admiral Thomas, came to Hawaii and declared that Hawaii's sovereignty had been restored. King Kamehameha III was so pleased that he presented Kearny with a handsome feather war cloak measuring four and a half feet by ten feet. It is said that it takes more than half a century to make a war cloak of this size.

Commodore Lawrence Kearny went on to serve in Norfolk, Virginia, and the New York Naval Shipyards. At home at the Kearny Cottage in Perth Amboy, Josephine had suffered an epileptic seizure and had fallen into the fireplace with the fire roaring. Two days later, on February 13, 1849, she tragically died from her wounds. John Michael died a year later on April 16, 1850. Louise and Mary Hall raised John Lawrence. Lawrence Kearny served as mayor of Perth Amboy in 1848 and 1849. He was a vestryman in St. Peter's Church from 1851 to 1855. He retired on November 14, 1861, and died in the cottage, the same house where he was born, on November 29, 1868, just shy of his seventy-ninth birthday. The USS *Kearny* is named in his honor. After the death of James Lawrence Kearny—the last direct descendant of Lawrence Kearny—in

1921, Kearny's beloved cottage was in danger of demolition. A group of concerned citizens headed by Judge Harold E. Pickersgill, who formed the Perth Amboy Historical Society, and Catherine McCormick decided to move Kearny's beloved home to Sadowski Parkway. The cottage was moved again in 1936 to its present site at 63 Catalpa Avenue. It is owned by the City of Perth Amboy and maintained by the Kearny Cottage Historical Society. One of Francis Kearny's engravings is located at the Kearny Cottage, as is other artwork from famous artists in Perth Amboy.

"It is not undue praise to say that Commodore Kearny stands as an example of what is [the] true claim to greatness of the United States Navy—its national character; it is of the people and for the people."[44]

Lawrence Kearny left a message in one of his last letters: "Woe to him who ventures upon the sacred soil, my old 'Cottage' and draws a nail. Inch by Inch shalt they weather-beaten sides bend to the blast and crack and split in very contempt of modern storms; and in humbleness of altitude they stand a monument of endurance."[45]

Chapter 5

THE DIRIGIBLE *AEREON* FLIES OVER PERTH AMBOY

June 1, 1863

Inventor, physician, politician, American Patriot." These are words that described Dr. Solomon Andrews (1806–1872), the first man in the world to steer an airship with any success. He did this at a time when the only means of air travel was a hot air balloon, which was prey to any wind that blew. Dr. Andrews was able to steer his dirigible regardless of the wind's direction, and he was even able to steer it directly against the wind. "You will seek his name in vain in the annals of aviation. But he and his amazing accomplishment live in dusty official documents, yellowed newspapers, and long forgotten letters in public and private files."[46]

Solomon Andrews was born on February 15, 1806, in Herkimer, New York. He was the son of Reverend Josiah Bishop Andrews, MD (March 17, 1775–April 26, 1853), born in Southington, Connecticut, and Mary Bissell (February 9, 1775–December 4, 1848), born in Windsor, Ontario, Canada. Reverend Josiah Andrews became a licentiate for gospel ministry on June 5, 1799. On April 12, 1802, he became the pastor in Killingworth, Connecticut. In 1811, he moved from Connecticut to New York City and started a school at 11 Sugar Loaf Street, which is now known as Franklin Street, and organized the first Sunday school in the area. The next year, he moved down the street to 20 and started the Scientific Institution, which prepared a class every year for college. He also supplied a church in Hempstead, Long Island, and preached there once a year. Dr. Josiah Bishop Andrews graduated from Yale in 1797 and the College of Physicians and Surgeons at New York City on March 11, 1816. He then moved to Perth Amboy, New Jersey, where he practiced medicine for thirteen years and was both a physician and a pastor at the Presbyterian church. He also was a health officer in Perth Amboy and president of the Medical Society of Middlesex County. In 1829, after the death of his father, Josiah moved back to Southington, Connecticut, to settle the estate. He would end up residing there for ten years and was made town representative in the state legislature in 1836. He later moved back to New York City and bought a house on Walker Street, where he practiced medicine. He died in New York at age seventy-eight. Josiah Bishop Andrews was a fine and noble-looking man. "His great aim was the acquirement and diffusion of knowledge. He was a man of great energy and perseverance. He had a large circle of friends who

Physician, inventor and politician, Dr. Solomon Andrews was the first man in the world to steer an airship with any success. *Courtesy of the Kearny Cottage Historical Society.*

appreciated his worth but also had envy from some bitter enemies among the clergy."[47]

Josiah and Mary had five children: an infant with no name who died at birth on July 4, 1803; Josiah Bissell, born July 24, 1804, left home and was lost at sea on July 27, 1825; Eliza, born January 14, 1808; William, who died as a child at age one in 1811; and Solomon, born February 15, 1806.

Influenced by his father's emphasis on education and following in his father's footsteps, Solomon Andrews graduated from Rutgers Medical School. He married Harriet Johnson of New York on October 13, 1829, and had seven children: Eliza Catharine, born July 27, 1830, died six years later on May 24, 1836; Harriet Cornelia, born June 16, 1832; Sarah Angelina, born November 20, 1833; Solomon Jr., born April 9, 1835; Joseph Bissell, born November 9, 1837, died June 6, 1848; Mary Eliza, born January 3, 1844; and James Green, born February 10, 1846.

Like his father, Solomon Andrews opened up a medical practice in Perth Amboy. Forever a tinkerer, Andrews was also an inventor. In 1849, he converted the pre–Revolutionary War barracks into the "Inventor's Institute," where he invented and patented many useful products. Its motto: "Without eccentricity there is no progression!"

In his youth at age seventeen, Solomon sat at the Presbyterian church where his father was pastor and gazed out the window to see an eagle soaring overhead. "As Solomon watched the bird winding its way across the sky he sat up, to use his own phrase, as though struck by 'an electric shock.' Henceforth he possessed but one great ambition and that was to construct an airship that would enable man to control his flight in the air as the eagle could."[48]

A friend once said of Solomon Andrews that "he could not examine a mechanism without seeing an improvement that might be made in it." Dr. Andrews thought about the concept of steering a balloon for years when he was a young man. His idea was to apply the principles of steering a sailboat to an airship. His theory is recognized today as an aerodynamic principle that is used by airplanes. As with a sailboat, the principle is that with a crosswind, the pressure of water is against the opposite side of the hull and the boat moves ahead when the hull is held at an angle. If you add the forces together, it gives a forward motion. In modern airplanes, the downward pull on a gliding plane is resisted by the air pressure underneath the wings. The forces combine to give a forward motion as the plane is set at a gliding angle.

Dr. Andrews theorized that with a balloon shaped like a cigar instead of a traditional round shape or, as he called it, a "flattened oblate spheroid," there is less resistance when moving than in a spherical balloon. From the balloon's pointed ends, he suspended a basket containing weight that could be moved from one end to the other end. This ability to shift the weight enabled him to maneuver the airship by controlling the angle of flight. Dr. Andrews calculated that an angle of ten to fifteen degrees would produce forward motion. He christened his ship the *Aereon*, which is Greek for "The Age of Air."

The *Aereon*'s balloons were over eighty feet long, twenty feet wide and ten feet deep. To store the craft, Andrews constructed the very first hangar bay, which was a building one hundred feet long, forty-six feet wide and thirty-six feet high. The airship was finished in the summer of 1849, but Andrews kept it in the hangar for five weeks to perfect his invention. He didn't take it into the air until later, probably due to errors in construction and other matters that occupied his attention.

As a physician and an inventor with twenty-four patents to his name, Dr. Solomon Andrews busied himself with his medical practice and other affairs. His most famous invention was the combination lock. Until Andrews's combination lock was invented, the bit of the key—the projecting part that operates the lock—was made with one piece with the shank or stem. Andrews invented a lock in which the shank was made in detachable sections and constructed the lock so that it could be worked only if the sections of the bit were slipped on the stem in a certain order. When the key was turned, the sections were removed and the lock could then be opened only by a person who knew the combination or the order in which the sections should be moved on the stem. So confident was Andrews that his lock would not be opened that he placed $1,000 in cash in a chest with the lock on it chained to a lamppost on the corner of Broad and Wall Streets in New York City. He welcomed anyone to the $1,000 if they could pick the lock. There were hundreds of takers, but none could open the lock. "The lock pickers were baffled. The chest was left chained to the post for a month and in that time hundreds of rival experts tried their hands at it and failed...This brought him fame and a slew of orders for bank locks and vault doors. In the next ten years, he

The first Yale lock invented by Solomon Andrews. This piece is located at the Kearny Cottage Museum, 63 Catalpa Avenue, Perth Amboy. *Photo by Paul W. Wang.*

supplied nearly two hundred banks from Maine to Mississippi and as far west as Michigan."[49]

In 1840, the United States Post Office Department requested an unpickable padlock for its mail sacks. By 1842, Andrews had produced and patented the lock. He held this contract with the U.S. Post Office Department for thirty years.

Andrews also invented a sewing machine, a barrel-making machine, fumigators, forging presses, a coal kitchen range, a wickless oil burner in which oil is converted to gas by the heat of its own flame and a nicotine-filtering pipe. He served as the president of the board of health, city councilman, justice of the peace and three times mayor of Perth Amboy. He designed Perth Amboy's sewer system, preventing disease and epidemics such as yellow fever and cholera.

New Jersey's first glimpse of Abraham Lincoln came on February 21, 1861, when the newly elected sixteenth president of the United States came to visit the state. The threat of Civil War was on everybody's mind. When the president arrived in New Brunswick, eyewitness Professor John C. Van Dyck (then a child of age five) sat perched on a box seat of his family's carriage. The train chugged across the bridge, snow blowing down onto the Raritan River, and then came to a halt. Professor Van Dyck gives his account of the incident:

> *There was a tremendous hurrah as the train came to a stop. Two men stepped onto the platform of the rear car, one the child's* [Van Dyck's] *father, the other a stranger. The child remembered:*
>
> *"A boy's father is always a big man to a boy. But that other man! What a giant he must be, I thought, for he was so much taller!…I do not remember what he said, if anything. He was there for only a few moments, and then the train moved off amid great shouts, the two men bowing from the platform until the train disappeared around the curve. The tall man was Abraham Lincoln. He was on his way to his first inauguration as President of the United States.*[50]

That April the Civil War had begun when Southern Rebels fired on Fort Sumter in Charleston Harbor. "A spirit of intense patriotism—a will to stand behind Lincoln and the Union, no matter what sacrifices were needed—swept across the county [Middlesex]."[51] During the Civil War, Andrews served as a Union physician. When he was at Harrison's Landing on the James River, he witnessed the newly incorporated Balloon Corps, whose responsibility was to observe enemy lines. Andrews believed that the *Aereon* would do a better job observing enemy lines than a hot air balloon.

In a letter dated August 9, 1862, Solomon Andrews wrote to President Abraham Lincoln about the *Aereon*. He pledged land valued at $50,000 for the success of the *Aereon* and promised to fly the airship five to ten miles into enemy territory and back again with no pay as demonstration of the soundness of the airship. To Andrews's dismay, Lincoln never answered the letter, and to this day no one knows why. Andrews wrote a second letter, this time to the secretary of war, Edward M. Stanton, who responded with a request for drawings and a description of the airship. Andrews promptly sent the requested information on September 1, 1862, to the Bureau of Topographic Engineers. The response was given in three days without Andrews being given a hearing. The bureau chief stated that he was "not fully convinced of the possibility of the method of locomotion." He then stated that the invention had no practical use. Solomon Andrews stated in reply, "I intend to build one immediately on my own account, and if successful I shall present it to the United States Government in the hope that it may shorten the War."[52]

Andrews had made improvements on his prototype from fourteen years ago. The gas was in three pointed cylinders, each thirteen by eighty feet, side by side and stiffened by lengthwise strips of wood. From the wood a basket was suspended that was twelve feet long and sixteen inches wide. This time, instead of an ordinary weight, it contained a car running on a track to permit shifting of the balance for angle control. Now the cylinders were divided into compartments in order to prevent the movement of the gas. The balloons were constructed out of 1,200 yards of Irish linen and 1,300 yards of cambric muslin for the gas containers. Dr. Andrews constructed the gas containers with his own invention—the varnishing machine. The balloons were sewn by the women of Perth Amboy. The balloons had a capacity of twenty-six thousand cubic feet and were filled with hydrogen.

On June 1, 1863, fifty-seven-year-old Dr. Solomon Andrews, who had never been in a hot air balloon in his life, piloted the *Aereon*. To get a feel

The dirigible *Aereon* flew over Perth Amboy on June 1, 1863. The balloons were constructed out of 1,200 yards of Irish linen and 1,300 yards of cambric muslin for the gas containers. The balloons had a capacity of twenty-six thousand cubic feet and were filled with hydrogen.

for what he accomplished, consider that the sides of the baskets were no higher than his knees. Despite all this going against him, Dr. Andrews flew the *Aereon* on its maiden voyage over Perth Amboy.

By August 1863, Dr. Andrews had gotten the kinks out of it. On August 6, 1863, he wrote to President Lincoln and to Secretary of War Stanton telling them what he had done and what he planned to do. "I propose to make a last trial of her power and then to destroy her. She can be balanced only when she is full of gas, and that is hazardous after ascending to a sufficient height to be out of the reach of bullets."[53] He continued in his letter, "Now all that I desire is that your Excellency will select some suitable person, the more scientific and practical the better, and send him here that he may examine the machine and witness the trial."[54] When nobody replied by September 4, 1863, Andrews decided to make his test flight.

The *New York Herald* wrote on September 8, 1863, "We have this week the pleasure to record the success of the most extraordinary invention of the age…at least the greatest stride in invention ever made by a single individual."[55] One witness would later state in a letter, "The Doctor sailed in any direction, either with, by or against the wind, the wind blowing from ten to fifteen miles an hour. He steered her as easily as a sailboat. He went off against the wind, turned her around, and came back from where he started."[56]

"After a few short flights, to satisfy himself and a few friends that all was right, he set her off in a spiral course upwards, she was going at a rate of not less than 120 miles per hour, and describing circles in the air of more than one and a half miles in circumference."[57] True to his word, Solomon Andrews destroyed the *Aereon*.

The test cost Solomon Andrews $10,000. Andrews went to Washington to see Abraham Lincoln. The president asked Andrews to back up what he said from reliable observers, so Andrews forwarded letters to the president from prominent Perth Amboy citizens. Lincoln never saw those letters. The War Department had become weary of Andrews and his dirigible and blocked his every move. Andrews went back to Washington to find his letters pigeonholed, although the secretary of war promised to show them to Lincoln. He never did. Andrews petitioned Congress to examine his invention, which was referred to the Military Affairs Committee. The War Department squashed that, but a statement landed on the desks of the senator and representatives who requested a demonstration of his invention with rubber miniatures in the basement of the Capitol. The Military Affairs Commission requested that the secretary of war appoint a commission to examine the *Aereon* and report. Joseph Henry, secretary of the Smithsonian Institute, headed the commission. Dr. Andrews appeared before the commission, and they liked the idea and recommended that Congress make appropriation. They did not receive the report until February 1865—nearly a year after requested. The Civil War was nearing a close, and there was no need for the *Aereon* as a spy vehicle.

However, the approval of Joseph Henry meant a lot to Andrews, and he set out to establish a company to transport people and merchandise by air between New York and Philadelphia. Henry stated that Andrews was "one of the most ingenious and successful inventors of this country."[58]

Unfortunately for Dr. Andrews, post–Civil War America was not a particularly good time to start a business. Reconstruction had started, and the economy was not doing very well. To add to Andrews's troubles, some people who were extremely religious believed that airship flight was sacrilegious. Despite this, in December 1865, Andrews formed the Aerial Navigation Company and built a new *Aereon #2*. This time it was made with two balloons eighty feet long, fifty feet wide and thirty-six feet deep with a capacity of sixty thousand cubic feet. While the ship of 1863 was sleek and cranky, this ship was too fat and stubby. There was not sufficient difference between vertical resistance and forward motion. The rudder often jammed. Despite this, the ship was ready in May 1866. On May 25, 1866, Andrews took off from Green and Houston Streets in New York, where the airship was built, and took three passengers: Dr. G. Waldo Hill, Charles M. Plumb and George W. Trow, the publisher of the famous *Trow's City Directory*. The *Aereon #2* landed safely in Astoria, Long Island. "Navigation of the air was a fixed fact. The problem of the centuries had been solved."[59]

With a new rudder and some other changes, the *Aereon #2* took off on June 5, 1866, this time with Charles M. Plumb the only passenger. The *Aereon #2* landed safely in Brookville, Long Island. But it would be the last flight of the *Aereon #2*. Postwar panic had swept the United States, and many banks went under, including the bank that backed the company. The organization was in debt and the stockholders unwilling to make up the deficit, so the Aerial Navigation Company went bankrupt.

Dr. Andrews eventually gave his patents to the nations of the world to benefit humanity. He died a few years later in 1872, his work forgotten.

Or was it? German Count Ferdinand von Zeppelin created his first prototype of the Zeppelin in the early 1900s, based on designs he had outlined in 1874 and detailed in 1893. He came over to the United States in 1863 to observe the military during the Civil War.

With the endorsement of German-born Carl Schurz, who was a general in the Union Army, and the support of others, Zeppelin received a pass signed by President Abraham Lincoln which enabled him to travel with the northern armies. After only a few months, however, Zeppelin left the war zone to explore the American frontier, and it was in St. Paul, Minnesota—far from the battlefields of the Civil War—that Zeppelin saw his first balloon…He went up in a balloon operated by John Steiner, a German-born balloonist who had served in the Union Army, the balloon reached 600 to 700 feet in a tethered ascent; Count von Zeppelin had seen the world from the air.[60]

Zeppelin would become fascinated with air travel just as Solomon Andrews was. There were reports of conversations Zeppelin had with Solomon Andrews about dirigibles when Zeppelin was in America. Did Solomon Andrews have any influence? Perhaps he did.

Chapter 6

Rebecca Spring

A Woman Ahead of Her Time
1811–1911

R ebecca Spring has been described in many ways but mostly as "a
curious blend of reformer, a conservative feminist, abolitionist,
transcendentalist and activist."[61] Rebecca was the fourth of seven children
born to Arnold Buffum and Rebecca Gould in Providence, Rhode
Island, on June 8, 1811. Arnold Buffum was an inventor, merchant and
the first president of the New England Anti-Slavery Society. He instilled
two primary values in all his children: education and abolition. The
family moved to Fall River, Massachusetts, in 1823, where the daughters
attended the Quaker-run Smithfield Academy. Rebecca belonged to
the Smithfield Female Mutual Improvement Society, a group that met
every week and read works of literature and discussed politics and ideals.
After graduating, Rebecca taught with her sisters Elizabeth and Lucy in
Fall River and Uxbridge. Then she taught at the Philadelphia Colored
School, a progressive institution that was totally integrated and coed.

Arnold Buffum took a trip to Europe and met Thomas Clarkson and
William Wilberface, who believed in the total abolition of slavery. When
Arnold returned, he started the first New England Anti-Slavery Society.
He eventually organized antislavery societies across New England. This
interested the Buffum daughters in abolitionism, and they distributed
pamphlets against slavery from house to house. They joined the Female

Rebecca Spring, "a curious blend of reformer, a conservative feminist, abolitionist, transcendentalist and activist." She and her husband, Marcus Spring, formed the Raritan Bay Union and its famous school, Eagleswood.

Anti-Slave Society. The activities of the society included petitioning Congress and raising money for food and clothing for runaway slaves.

Rebecca's view of slavery was further fueled when, in 1838, she attended the Women's Anti-Slavery Convention in Pennsylvania. This was not before Rebecca married Marcus Spring on October 26, 1836. Spring was born on October 21, 1810, in Northbridge, Massachusetts. He was a Unitarian and self-made man and an advocate for the factory class. He also aided many runaway slaves. "Marcus Spring shared Rebecca's concern to improve living standards for the urban poor."[62]

The marriage of Rebecca and Marcus was considered "romantic, compassionate, and egalitarian." It was unusual in the male-dominated society of Victorian America for a couple to believe in spiritual equality of the sexes. In Victorian times, men and women lived in different worlds. Despite what was considered "proper," the couple often referred to each other affectionately. Rebecca often referred to Marcus as "my precious one, my husband and dearest friend."[63] Marcus was equally as affectionate. They made frequent trips to Europe and had a list of family, friends and acquaintances that made up a who's who of the nineteenth century, including Rebecca's sister Elizabeth Buffum Chace, who was a lecturer in Europe and America and was active in prison reform, pacifism, abolitionism and suffrage. Other friends of the Springs included Bronson Alcott, William and Mary Howitt, Charles Dickens, Ralph Waldo Emerson, Henry David Thoreau and William Wordsworth. Rebecca was also a good friend of the Transcendentalist writer Margaret Fuller, arch-feminist and editor of the *Dial*.

Of all Rebecca Spring's progressive beliefs, the one she felt most passionate about was abolitionism. Although her father instilled her initial abolitionist beliefs, an 1852 trip to Cuba and South Carolina left her revolted at the conditions in which slaves were kept. She felt especially strongly about how female slaves were treated. "Motherhood was an essential element of True Womanhood; in separating slave mothers from their children, using them as 'breeders,' or forcing them to work during pregnancy at dangerous risk to the child they were carrying, slave owners—in the abolitionist view—proved themselves enemies of the social order."[64]

"At the time there was also awakening interest in women's rights, suffrage, prison reform, and the redistribution of wealth, concern with factory conditions, physical fitness, hygiene, phrenology, temperance, experiments in community living, and various shortcuts to salvation."[65] Rebecca believed that the plight of the slave was similar to that of the situation of nineteenth-century women. She felt that women were under subjugation just like slaves. "Marcus and Rebecca were themselves receptive to liberal ideas and stirred by the concepts and philosophies which lay behind them; to some they were radical, to some liberal, to others merely humanitarian."[66]

In 1843, Marcus Spring, along with Albert Brisbane and Horace Greeley, purchased 613 acres of land that became the North American Phalanx, where they were chief stockholders. This community was famous for its products, which included wheat, rye, buckwheat, flour, mustard and cornmeal. These products became well known, especially in New York. The North American Phalanx produced the first boxed cereal in the United States. But a discord among the North American Phalanx and thirty families followed the Springs to their new community.

In 1853, the Springs moved to Perth Amboy, New Jersey. They purchased a 268-acre piece of land and formed the Raritan Bay Union, a utopian community that prided itself on education and abolitionism. They christened the estate and school Eagleswood. "Building materials were cheap, labor was plentiful, and it was a small matter to run up something which would have practical value in one way or another."[67]

"They combined vision with practical experience and a certain amount of horse sense, and apparently both of them were able to inspire confidence, trust, and affection during a period of ferment when these attributes were expected to be but often were not common currency."[68]

A few friends who desire a higher form of Union in Industry, Education and Social Life than is found in existing society have secured a position at the mouth of the Raritan River, near Perth Amboy, New Jersey, where they purpose unpledged to any social theory as yet presented practically to apply such principles of Joint Stock Association as commend themselves to conscience and common sense. The domain consisting of two hundred and seventy acres of fertile and easily cultivated land well watered healthy, open to the sea air and combining rare beauty with unsurpassed business advantage, is easy of access from New York and Philadelphia, and presents every needed facility for safe and cheap transportation of produce goods and manufactures.[69]

Education of both sexes was emphasized throughout the Raritan Bay Union. Both white and black students were taught in the same classrooms:

Education will be accessible to all the children of members; and as many children from abroad will be received as the limits of the Union will permit; and the hope is, to surround the pupils with such an atmosphere of friendly and parental guardian ship as will, to a high degree ensure their health, purity, and symmetric growth.[70]

Although it only survived economically until 1857, the Raritan Bay Union achieved great educational prowess. The school overshadowed the

Above left: Angelina Grimke was married to Theodore Weld, who was headmaster at Eagleswood.

Above right: Sarah Grimke, sister to Angelina Grimke. Both women taught at Eagleswood and loved to shop in Perth Amboy in bloomers.

Union itself. Theodore Weld was the principal. Both men and women taught at Eagleswood. The faculty included Weld's wife, Angelina Grimke, and her sister Sarah M. Grimke. (Both were addicted to bloomers and would shop in Perth Amboy in them, to the dismay of some of the local populace.) The Grimke sisters and Weld would teach at Eagleswood for almost ten years. The coed school encouraged girls to speak at public gatherings, act in plays and participate and excel in athletics. "The school was attended mostly by Southern children who paid $300 a semester for a regular course of study and five dollars for each language. Music, drawing and painting instruction each cost $20 extra."[71]

They sat through endless sermons, lectures, discussions, and debates, read the papers and periodicals, the tracts and pamphlets, and listened with attentive ears and open minds to the advocacies of the Quakers and the Shakers, the Congregationalists and Unitarians, the Transcendentalists, the Garrisonians, the Mormons, the Millerites, and the Rappites, to all those who had beliefs and messages of one sort or another however old, however new.[72]

The Springs' idealism extended to their abolitionist beliefs. When John Brown attacked the federal arsenal at Harpers Ferry, Virginia, in 1859, he was arrested along with his raiders. Rebecca Spring wrote to John Brown and went to visit him in his Virginia prison. "We have talked against slavery all these years, now somebody has done something. These men have risked their lives. I must go."[73]

Rebecca Spring had an unusual view of violence: "When men fight and hurt each other, women should go and take care of them."[74] She consoled John Brown in prison and petitioned for his release. She was denied, but she did promise and deliver the burial on free northern ground for two raiders, Absalom G. Haslett and Aaron Dwight Stevens. After the two raiders were executed, their bodies were sent to New Jersey. "As the bodies were being shipped north, the Springs learned that an angry crowd planned to assemble in Perth Amboy and throw the bodies into the bay. The bodies were taken to Rahway and secretly brought to Eagleswood where they were buried."[75] They were later moved in 1899 to North Elba, New York, to lie next to John Brown's homestead.

What works in theory does not necessarily work in practice, and in reality, Eagleswood was not the utopia it promised to be. Not everyone agreed with the Springs' idealistic view of Eagleswood. "In 1856 Henry Thoreau visited the community to give lectures and to survey the land. He described it later as a colony of radical opinions and old-fashioned culture."[76] Thoreau was not the only one with an unfavorable opinion of the community: "A later feminine visitor was impressed by the beauty of the grounds, but complained that 'in the house, it is the same as everywhere; all have so much to do, there is no time for amusement; they do not even meet together in the evenings except occasionally, each family occupying its own rooms as though they were in separate houses.'"[77]

During the Civil War, enrollment at Eagleswood dwindled. This is primarily due to the fact that the majority of the students were southerners and were unable to make the trip to New Jersey. To help the war effort, the Springs converted Eagleswood into a military academy "for the cause of freedom." Rebecca Spring personally supervised the strict codes of religious and moral discipline enforced at Eagleswood.

She also established an art colony at Eagleswood that hosted artists such as George Inness, Louis Tiffany and William Page. It was at this time that the Springs also supported a school for children of slaves, along with supplying food for the increasing number of runaway slaves traveling north due to the Emancipation Proclamation. In addition, the Springs established an Underground Railroad stop at Eagleswood.

The Springs grew weary of Eagleswood by the late 1860s and closed its doors in 1868. The Springs now concentrated on family and dedicated their time to their children. Tragedy struck when Marcus Spring died unexpectedly in 1874. Thirty carriages were at his funeral procession. He is buried in Alpine Cemetery in Perth Amboy. After Marcus died, a distraught Rebecca moved to California with her children, and the Eagleswood property was passed down to an insurance company in 1888. In 1912, the Pardee Tile Company bought the remaining eight acres of land and remained there until shortly before World War II. In her later years, Rebecca often thought of Eagleswood: "I look back and see a light that went out from it—small, but bright and pure and true. I believe some holy work is yet to be done through our Eagleswood."[78] Rebecca Spring died in 1911 in California. Her unpublished biography, "A Book of Remembrance," is located at Stanford University in Stanford, California.

Chapter 7

THOMAS MUNDY PETERSON'S HISTORIC VOTE

March 31, 1870

Thomas Mundy Peterson was born in Metuchen, New Jersey, on October 6, 1824, the son of parents who had been slaves to the Mundy family; thus, he was often called Thomas Mundy. His father was Thomas Peterson, whose parents were free. His mother was Lucy Green, whose parents were slaves for Governor William Augustus Newell's family. Newell was governor of New Jersey from 1857 to 1860. Thomas Mundy Peterson's parents came to Perth Amboy in 1828, when Thomas was four years old. On February 10, 1844, Thomas Peterson married Daphne Reeve, whose family had been slaves on the Bell estate in Perth Amboy.

On March 30, 1870, the Fifteenth Amendment to the federal Constitution had just been adopted by Congress, allowing Thomas Peterson, an African American, to vote. There happened to be an election the following day in Perth Amboy. In an interview from an undated newspaper clipping (circa 1877–84) in the possession of Mrs. Johannes Garretson Koyler, Thomas Mundy Peterson stated, "I was working for Mr. J.L. Kearny on the morning the day of the election and did not think of voting until he came out to the stable where I was attending to the horses and advised me to go to the polls and exercise a citizen's privilege…When I went home to dinner at noon I met Mr. Marcus Spring

Thomas Mundy Peterson, the first black voter under the Fifteenth Amendment. Peterson was encouraged to vote by James Lawrence Kearny. *Courtesy of Perth Amboy Free Public Library.*

Son of Lawrence Kearny, James Lawrence Kearny became a prominent citizen in Perth Amboy. He encouraged Thomas Mundy Peterson to vote in the election of March 31, 1870, in Perth Amboy. *Courtesy of the Kearny Cottage Historical Society.*

of Eagleswood, a place about a mile out of town and he, too, advised me to claim the right of suffrage at the polls."[79]

While walking up High Street heading for the old Paterson Home, Thomas Peterson approached city hall, and James Lawrence Kearny called to him from the window and asked him if he wanted to vote. Peterson stated that he did wish to vote but only if the amendment was adopted. Thomas Peterson did not have to concern himself; the amendment had been adopted.

On March 31, 1870, Perth Amboy had a special election to decide whether or not to adopt a new charter. Some people in town wanted to revise the present charter, while others wished to drop the present city charter altogether and revert to a township form of government. Thomas Peterson recalls, "As I advanced to the polls one man offered me a ticket bearing the words 'revised charter' and another one marked, 'no charter.' I thought I would not vote to give up our charter after holding it for so long; so I chose a revised charter ballot." He handed the ballot to Patrick Convery. "Our side won the election by a vote of 230 to 63 and I may mention as a coincidence that I was afterward appointed one of a committee of seven to revise the charter."[80]

Eleven years after Thomas Peterson cast his vote in Perth Amboy, the question arose as to whether he was actually the first African American voter in the United States. Thomas Mundy Peterson came to James Lawrence Kearny, Patrick Convery, William Paterson (former mayor) John Fothergill (former mayor) and I.T. Golding (city treasurer) to form a committee to verify if this was true because he did not want the honor if it was not so. The committee investigated for months for all thirty-eight states and ten territories at the time. Only five states had elections that day, and in those elections, no African Americans voted in four of them. Therefore, there was no question that Thomas Mundy Peterson had cast that historic vote in Perth Amboy on March 31, 1870.

On Memorial Day, May 30, 1884 (then known as Decoration Day), a mass meeting was held in city hall, which was filled to capacity with Perth Amboy's citizens. James A. Chapman, former mayor of Perth Amboy, presided. James Lawrence Kearny then presented Thomas Mundy Peterson with the Abraham Lincoln Gold Medal. It had a profile of Abraham Lincoln on one side and on the reverse side was inscribed the following:

Presented By Citizens of Perth Amboy, N.J.
To
Thomas Peterson
The First Colored Voter in the United States
Under The Fifteenth Amendment
At An Election Held In That City
MARCH 31, 1870

Thomas Peterson never felt like he was completely dressed unless he wore his medal on his coat and over his heart. He faithfully attended services every week at St. Peter's Episcopal Church in Perth Amboy and was a custodian at Perth Amboy Elementary School No. 1 from 1870 to 1877. Active in the Republican Party, he was once a delegate at the Republican county convention and was Perth Amboy's first African American to hold elected office on the Middlesex County Commission. He was also the first African American from Perth Amboy to serve on a jury.

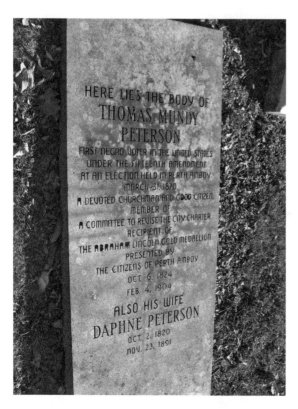

Peterson was buried in St. Peter's Episcopal Church Cemetery. Buried with him is his wife, Daphne Peterson. *Photo by the author.*

Thomas Mundy Peterson died on February 4, 1904, and he is buried in St. Peter's Cemetery. Judge Harold Pickersgill owned the medal of honor after Peterson's death. Reverend George H. Boyd tried to buy it from him for St. Peter's Church, but Pickersgill refused to sell it even though Boyd offered a large sum for it. It was later sold in an auction in New York and finally sold to Xavier University, an African American Catholic institution in New Orleans.

In New Jersey, March 31 is annually celebrated as Thomas Mundy Peterson Day in recognition of his historic vote. In Perth Amboy, Elementary School No. 1 was once called Thomas Mundy Peterson School in his honor. It now serves as an annex to William C. McGinnis Middle School located on State Street.

Chapter 8

TRAGEDY ON MARKET STREET

June 15, 1921

It was just before 6:00 p.m. when a fire alarm went off in Herman Rudderman's junkyard shop, the Perth Amboy Iron and Metal Company, on South Second Street. A wastepaper basket had caught on fire. Probably someone threw out a cigarette or live ashes into the wastebasket, but no one knows for sure. Neither does anyone know why someone in the office didn't put out the fire himself, but the alarm went through to the Davison Avenue firehouse. The volunteer firemen leaped into action as soon as the alarm went off. "Torgenson leaped to the wheel, Finan cranked the engine of the combination hose truck and chemical wagon and Kafton, assistant foreman in charge of the truck, as he sprang to the last place on the running board, shouted: 'Let her roll!'"[81] The Eagle Hose and Chemical Company took off.

In 1921, the firehouse was located on Davison Avenue, which at the time was five blocks west of the railroad tracks. The railroad crossing was located between Elm Street and South Second Street, and the tracks were street level and monitored by a crossing watchman. The truck sped east down Market Street toward the crossing used by both the Central and Pennsylvania's Long Branch Line. As the fire truck approached the crossing, the driver saw three automobiles that were stopped on the near side. No one knows why they were stopped; they either saw the

On June 15, 1921, nine members of the Eagle Hose and Chemical Company met their fate when their fire truck hit a passing train through town. The crossing guard had left the gates open, resulting in the tragedy. *Courtesy of the Massopust family.*

oncoming train bound for Lakewood and Barnegat or they had halted for the approaching fire truck. The fire truck's driver, John Torgenson, thought they had pulled over for the fire truck, so he swung the truck over to the right to avoid the cars.

The crossing watchman, Andrew Thomas, was a sixty-four-year-old Slav immigrant who spoke little English. In his hut, Thomas saw the train four blocks away, and the ringing of the crossing bell further warned him of the approaching train. Then he heard the clang of the oncoming fire truck. According to the rules of the time, in a situation such as this one, the watchman was supposed to close the gates and then rush out to flag the fire truck and, if there was still time left, flag the train. The watchman did not follow procedure, nor did he use his head during the emergency. The train was far enough away that there was time that it could have been flagged down by standing on a nearby ladder used for an overhead signal tower. The watchman did not do this either. Instead, he snatched his red flag and dashed toward the oncoming firemen, leaving the gates wide open.

Torgenson never knew what hit him. Andrew Kafton was the only one who saw the train coming, and he shouted, "Jump for our lives!"[82] as he glimpsed the locomotive bearing down upon the fire truck. Kafton rolled off the truck and Joseph Finan followed, as did two other firemen. Kafton rolled but stopped just before he was against the engine. Finan stopped, rolling as his body hit the chief's.

Everyone in the area heard a load roar as the fire truck grazed the engine and then hit the locomotive in the combination baggage and smoker car. The truck recoiled, and then it hit one of the crossing gates. Mutilated bodies were carried three hundred feet down the track before they were churned free. Then the train came to a halt. The fire truck hit the tank of Engine 581 just above the journal box and the front of car 313. Andrew Thomas was caught between the truck and the crossing gate but survived.

Both Joseph Finan and Andrew Kafton, although injured, lived to tell the tale of the crash and clearly stated that the gates were up. Finan stated, "I did not see the flagman…until we had passed the automobile in front of us. I jumped and in doing so bumped into Kafton and rolled in the roadbed with him."[83]

One of the witnesses was Dr. Andrew Loblein of New Brunswick.

According to Dr. Loblein, he was going west on Market Street, in the opposite direction from the fire truck and as the gates were up proceeded to cross the tracks. He said he saw no fireman or any red flag, but when his car reached the tracks he saw the express almost upon him. He stepped on the accelerator, he said, not believing he could escape being hit but luckily beat the train. He said he had no more than crossed the tracks when the fire engine passed him going at a terrific rate of sped. He said he thought it was making about fifty miles an hour and believed the train was going just as fast…Realizing that a crash could not be avoided. Dr. Loblein said he jammed on his brakes and looked through the rear windows of his car just in time to see the crash. There was a deafening noise, he said and then he witnessed the most horrible occurrence he had ever seen.[84]

Among the dead were Hans Holt, John Donegan, Joseph Kutcher, James Anderson, John Torgenson and L. Peter Larson. Victor Jandrup,

Jack Mowery and George F. Larson would die in the hospital the next day. Among the injured were Edward V. Johnson, Ralph Paulsen, Joseph Finan and Andrew Kafton. The Larson brothers left behind a number of children. Morgan T. Larson (governor of New Jersey from 1929 to 1932) took them in and raised them in his house on High Street.

Eight years old at the time, Arthur Brown was not certain if his father, volunteer fireman Joseph Brown, was on the truck. Joseph Brown was working all night at his father's farm, and Arthur was not sure if his father had gotten back. Joseph Brown often stopped at the firehouse after he returned from his father's farm, and someone had said that he was on the truck. To his relief, Arthur saw his father walking down Watson Avenue. He had gotten off the bus at Prospect Street coming back from his father's farm. Joseph Brown later found out that he was in charge of the funerals. There was a prayer service at Eagle Fire House led by Mayor William C. Wilson, himself a charter member of Eagle Hose and Chemical Company. "He prayed for the recovery of the injured and the repose of the dead firemen."[85] A relief fund was started for the families of the nine men who had died so terribly. It was well responded to. "Over $18,000 was raised in the city by popular subscription and was divided among the widows and dependents of the dead and injured firemen."[86]

The engineer, Theodore Brown, and the conductor, Arthur A. Ridgeway of Barnegat, were arrested on the charge of manslaughter, and Andrew Thomas was also arrested for manslaughter while still in

Eight years old at the time of the tragedy, Arthur Brown was not certain if his father, volunteer fireman Joseph Brown, was on the truck that hit the train. To his relief, Arthur saw his father walking down Watson Avenue that morning. This photo was taken in 2009 at the Firemen's Convention in Wildwood, New Jersey. *Photo by the author.*

Located in Alpine Cemetery, local firefighters place a wreath for their fallen brothers every May around Memorial Day. The memorial honors the nine men who tragically lost their lives that fateful day and all the fallen firefighters of Perth Amboy. *Photo by the author.*

the hospital. "The engineer when questioned by the authorities, it is claimed, stated the gates were not down."[87] Moreover, the train was speeding at forty miles per hour, considered too fast to go through a town.

An ordinance was passed the next day to limit the speed of trains passing through town to ten miles per hour. The final solution came when the old train station building was moved to 210 Lewis Street. The building was sold to William Michael Stonaker, a track foreman for the Central Railroad of New Jersey, who saved it. The building is three stories tall with four high dormer windows and is an exact replica of many other train stations. In 1923, a new train station was built on Market Street where the old one originally stood, and the tracks were lowered to avoid such accidents. During the late 1990s and early 2000s, the train station got a face-lift thanks to a grant from former New Jersey governor Christine Todd Whitman (1994–2001) and Senator Frank R. Lautenberg (1982–2001, 2003–present).

There is a Firemen's Monument at Alpine Cemetery at 703 Amboy Avenue to commemorate the nine firemen who died so tragically. It is a walrus-mustached fireman in full gear holding the nozzle of a hose.

Arthur Brown remembers, "And all because of a wastepaper basket on fire."

Chapter 9

THE KU KLUX KLAN RIOTS

June 5, 1923, and August 30, 1923

The Ku Klux Klan never had the power it craved. It had little to no success in influencing elections, nor did it have any political persuasion, nor was it ever successful in state politics. "Yet all the publicity and the Klan's alleged power, the organization was not really successful. It never played a crucial role in a national election, never decisively influenced a national political convention, and was not particularly successful in state politics."[88]

However, on a local level, the Klan was a potent political force. Many New Jersey communities in the 1920s had Klansmen for leaders. It was during this time that the Ku Klux Klan wished to recruit members in the East. The Klan made its appeal across the New Jersey/New York area and to many cities in the surrounding vicinity. Klan members were found in Passaic, Bergen, Essex, Union and Morris Counties in New Jersey. It was the Klan's impression that closely built-up residential cities were more "Klan friendly." The Ku Klux Klan prides itself on standing up for white supremacy, the separation of church and state and keeping law and order. It supposedly stands for traditional American values, including Protestant fundamentalism and prohibition. It also believes in opposition to the Catholic Church. Because of the prohibition issues in a less-than-dry New Jersey filled with foreign immigrants, the Klan viewed New

Jersey as somewhat of a problem. It is for this reason that it concentrated on recruitment in New Jersey. Drafting of Klansmen continued in New Jersey until 1923—when the Klan decided to come to Perth Amboy.

In 1923, Perth Amboy was (as it still is today) a multiracial and religious-oriented community with local residents consisting mostly of immigrants or descendants of immigrants. This mixed population included growing immigrant groups such as Poles, Russians, Hungarians, Czechs, Jews, Italians and the old immigrants of Irish, Germans, Danish, as well as African Americans and the white Protestants in the city; 72 percent of the population was foreign born or first-generation Americans. High, middle and lower classes all mingled on the streets together.

The Klan decided to send recruiters to Perth Amboy in May 1923. Few people in Perth Amboy were interested, so the Klan decided to have a secret meeting. Members sent out letters at their Point Pleasant meeting to generate interest. The letters had no letterhead and were signed "The Committee." But it was no secret—everyone knew who they were from.

The Klan began its meeting as planned in the Junior Hall on Smith Street on June 5, 1923. The Klan's famous speaker, Dr. Oscar Haywood, onetime Baptist minister in New York, opened the meeting at 9:50 p.m. A crowd of 2,500 people gathered outside in protest. This crowd consisted of multiple ethnicities, all of whom came out of their homes to fight the Klan. As the meeting began, the shades went down and there was silence for thirty minutes. The crowd lost patience and stormed the building, pushing its way past the guards. Haywood began speaking, stating that "Jews were aliens" and that Jews and Catholics were "unworthy of American nationality."

At this statement, the crowd inside the hall headed for Haywood, shouting profanities at him. Several men jumped onto the platform and attempted to seize him. The police set up a decoy paddy wagon and backed it up to the front door while Haywood was smuggled out the back into a taxi. This escape was almost botched because the taxi ran out of gas two blocks down the street. But no one noticed the vehicle, and it was immediately refueled and Haywood was escorted to the Rahway train station, from where he went to New York City. Haywood later commented that he was never in his life heckled or treated the way he was by the people of Perth Amboy at any Klan-sponsored event.

It took the police one hour to disperse the crowd. Some windows were broken, some flower beds upturned, some garbage cans knocked over and some cars broken into. Other than that, there was minimal property damage. The *New York Times* stated that the Klan received "nothing more that it deserved in its attempt to recruit in Perth Amboy."[89]

The Klan protested to Perth Amboy's mayor, William C. Wilson, to no avail. Its members then demanded that New Jersey governor George Silzer apprehend two officers of the Knights of Columbus and a Perth Amboy banker whom they believed stirred the people. Governor Silzer ignored these pleas and stated that he was not interested in meeting with masked groups. He would, however, meet with Klan leaders if they unmasked. The Klan refused his offer.

Despite the resistance offered by the people of Perth Amboy, the Klan decided to come back in August. The Klan decided to do this to "defend their honor" from the previous fiasco. This time, Klansmen boldly distributed handbills and flyers and nailed up posters everywhere. When word got out that the Klan was coming back to Perth Amboy, this angered the residents. Some children were so terrified that they hid under their beds. The people of Perth Amboy were not going to stand for this.

On Thursday, August 30, 1923, the meeting started at 6:00 p.m. as scheduled at the Odd Fellows Hall located on lower Smith Street. Free hot dogs were offered to potential members. The Klan had brought about one hundred armed bodyguards, and six police officers were also assigned to guard the meeting.

The Knights of Columbus and the Free Masons decided that they were going to do something about the Klan. They met on Hobart Street and took bricks from St. Mary's Church Rectory on Center Street and the Leon Building on the corner of Smith Street and King Street (which were under construction at the time). They then decided to march on the building. In an effort to gain entrance, they threw the bricks through the meeting hall and broke every window in the building. The mob also broke some of the windows in the surrounding buildings. The eastern plate at the window of Gannon & Sheehy Furnishing Store was broken.

The crowd gathered between 6:00 p.m. and 8:00 p.m. and tried to gain access to the hall. They were repelled by a dozen of the armed Klansmen and six policemen armed only with nightsticks. All off-duty policemen were ordered to report to the Odd Fellows Hall at once. Since it was summertime and many were busy, they were slow in responding.

One Klansman, Harold R. Moford of New Monmouth, flashed a gun in the air and exchanged words with the crowd, and the first rush of the hall started. The crowd got to Moford, and some blows were thrown at him. Motorcycle Officer Layden and Detective Gutowski got to him in time, confiscated his .38 gun and took him right to the station.

At 8:30 p.m., tear gas was thrown at the crowd, but the smoke and fumes had only a one-minute effect. Tear gas was then thrown a number of times at the crowd, which at one point reached more than six thousand people. The tear gas was deemed ineffective.

Police Chief Niels J. Tonnesen ordered some paddy wagons to the scene to evacuate the Klansmen and their sympathizers. They were taken out the back doors, bundled and put into the waiting police vans.

Niels J. Tonnesen was police chief during the 1923 KKK riots in Perth Amboy. Under his command, no one was killed in the riots, and the police department acted admirably. *Courtesy of Donna Ross.*

The mob got wind of this and went in the back of the building, brushed the police away and beat the Klansmen inside the wagons.

Chief Tonnesen had no choice but to call the state police at 9:15 p.m. Seven officers from Morgan and Freehold were each issued with nightsticks, a supply of ammunition and a regular revolver. They traveled at a rate over sixty miles per hour. It was the first time in Perth Amboy history that the state police were called in to help quiet a riot. When they arrived at 9:30 p.m., they came tearing down Smith Street; the rioters simply removed the state police from their motorcycles and pinned them in nearby doorways.

Still unable to gain access, the anti-Klan mob then placed straw in front of the building and prepared to burn down the hall. One of these

William "Wild Bill" Hallahan, my great-grandfather (my father's maternal grandfather), drove the family car into the Odd Fellows Hall, allowing the mob access to the Klan meeting. *Courtesy of the Massopust family.*

citizens was my great-grandfather, William Hallahan. Concerned for his mother-in-law, who lived nearby, William "Wild Bill" Hallahan decided that burning down the hall was not a good idea, so he got his car, started up King Street and rammed it through the hall door, jumping out at the last minute and in the processes destroying the door and allowing entrance into the building.[90]

The crowd members then stormed the hall chasing after the hapless Klansmen. They pursued them all over the streets and pulled off the hoods of any Klansman they caught. Some of the Klansmen took off their own hoods and ran out the door in an effort to escape. This did not stop the mob. Any person from out of town was taken and dealt with. Anyone with an out-of-town license plate had his tires slashed. Carloads of Klansmen made a break for it. The anti-Klan mob ran after the Klansmen, grabbed them and placed their heads in the sewers until they gurgled. The Klansmen ran for their lives. They were stopped halfway down Smith Street, and the Klansmen were severely beaten and their car set ablaze. It has been said that some of the Klansmen were chased out of town by armed citizens and shot at as they left.

When the mob reached the Odd Fellows Hall, they found out that members of the Valhalla Lodge of Odd Fellows had assembled for their meeting. "A member of the lodge in the Anti-Klan mob conversed with one of his brother members and when it was found that they were not connected with the Klan meeting so the crowd was told to allow the Odd Fellows to depart through the fire escape and through the backyard unharmed."[91]

At 10:00 p.m., Chief Tonnesen decided to call in a second riot call. A mistake in sounding the call resulted in an alarm being sent in from alarm box 25 at the Central Railroad and Smith Street. When the fire department arrived, Chief John Campbell found out that the box had not been opened and the alarm had been sent in by the police station. All the tear gas made it seem like there was smoke on King Street. The fire alarm and riot call brought more people out of their homes.

The fire department went to help with the riot. Helmeted police officers clubbed through the crowd so the fire department could connect its hoses, but the mob got back together and chopped up the hoses with knives and axes. After reinforcements of the state troopers arrived, the police tried getting the Klansmen out off the rooftops to unmarked cars waiting below. These cars never made it out of town. They were stopped, the occupants taken and beaten and the cars turned over and set on fire. Rocks and bottles were thrown at the Klansmen.

The police then ordered Smith Street and King Street to be cleared so they could get patrol cars to get the Klan members out. Ten motorcycle policemen cleared the road. The crowd then rushed in and threw stones and bricks at the police. The stone throwing was so brutal that the lives of the patrolmen were in danger, so the police pulled back.

Fifty Klansmen and sympathizers were removed by the police between 10:00 p.m. and 11:30 p.m. They were forced to wait at the station until Tonnesen thought they were safe. Later that night, the patrol wagons unloaded the Klansmen on Penn Street and Jefferson Street, where they were left by the police patrol to fend for themselves. They reportedly found their tires slashed and were chased through the streets by the remaining anti-Klan mob.

The anti-Klan mob was stationed at the end of the city line on New Brunswick Avenue to the other side of the city line, making it impossible for the Klansmen to escape in automobiles. "In a majority of the cases after beatings were administered, tires were cut and other damage was inflicted making it impossible for visitors to continue on their way."[92] That night, the crowd began finding every out-of-town car and slashing its tires. They overturned and burned the cars. Two suspected vehicles were pushed into the Raritan River. No Klansman escaped a beating. At 1:30 a.m., the crowd on Smith Street made a circle out of cloth and tied it around a tire rim, soaked it in gasoline and then set it on fire. The circle is the anti-Klan symbol.

Around 5:00 a.m., the town settled back down. About ten individuals in the mob suffered injuries. Only one policeman was injured: Officer James Egan was hit behind the ear with a stone. No one was killed. Mayor William C. Wilson had little comment about the riot. He was out of town at the time fishing and had slept through the incident, stating, "We will allow no more meetings without permits."[93] New Jersey governor George Sebastian Silzer stated that it was "purely a local matter."[94] Chief Tonnesen and several police officers were almost indicted for failure to respond immediately to the scene and for allowing the riot to reach such violent proportions. The Klansmen testified, complaining about the incident. After hours of testimony, the grand jury decided not to indict the Perth Amboy police, stating that no one was killed and the police department had acted admirably.

This was the beginning of the decline of Klan influence in New Jersey. Word spread about the riot, and the Klan lost whatever power it had in New Jersey as its New Jersey membership diminished. The people of Perth Amboy had united to strike back against bigotry. One thing is for certain—the Ku Klux Klan never came back to Perth Amboy again.

Chapter 10

AMERICA ON WHEELS

The Perth Amboy Arena
1939–1949

O ne of Perth Amboy's hidden treasures lies in the memories of individuals who had the pleasure of roller-skating in the Perth Amboy Arena. It was a grand building located off Smith Street on Herbert Street. The huge arena took up the entire block with a parking lot that extended to Market Street. For ten years, the rink delighted patrons from all over New Jersey, New York and the surrounding area. The building had once been an old factory that manufactured biplanes for a military contract for use in World War I. After the war was over, the factory closed down and the building was converted to a roller rink by the late 1930s. Part of the America on Wheels Chain, the building had two entrances, two ticket takers and an enormous parking lot that extended from Smith Street down to Market Street with a capacity of over four hundred cars, complete with a parking lot attendant who told you where to park. The front of the arena was gravel covered and also allowed for parking.

On the right-hand side of the arena were the skate rooms, which were men's and ladies' dressing rooms, and the cloak room. On the left-hand side of the arena were offices for the manager and rink administration and the concession stand for the patrons' convenience. In the far back on the left-hand side were men's and ladies' restrooms, which were over

The largest roller rink in the world was located on Smith and Herbert Streets in Perth Amboy. Part of the America on Wheels chain, the building had two entrances, two ticket takers and an enormous parking lot that extended to Market Street. *Courtesy of Chester Freid.*

twenty-five feet long, with attendants that handed you a towel. The rink had over forty skate boys employed at once. The building had two levels. On the second level on a loft above the front entrance was a live organist who entertained the patrons as they skated.

The huge arena included a full acre of maple flooring, the largest in the world at its time. The building was over 220 feet long from front to back and over 150 feet wide. It was so huge that it had six large pillars (three on the right center and three on the left center) that supported the building. It was a majestic site to behold.

To the delight of many patrons, the roller rink in Perth Amboy opened its doors to the public on Christmas Day 1939. For twenty-five cents, one could skate for three and a half hours—the rink was open from 7:30 p.m. to 11:00 p.m. If there was a party or special event, the rink was open until midnight. A group lesson cost ten cents a person. A hot dog was fifteen cents, and a Coke was ten cents.

Skating is a sport that boys, girls, men and women can all enjoy at any age without being considered too masculine or too feminine, nor is it delegated to the very young, for one is never considered to be too old to

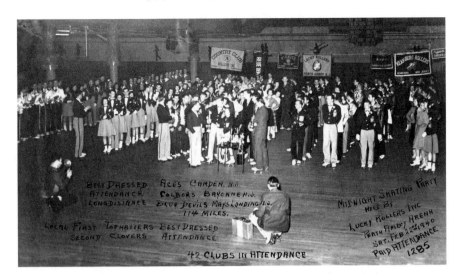

The interior of the America on Wheels Perth Amboy Arena shows the building's capacity of holding volumes of people, as at this party. *Courtesy of Chester Freid.*

begin skating. It is an ageless, genderless, timeless sport that anyone can enjoy and start at any age with no shame or ridicule. It also is a relatively inexpensive sport to participate in, which makes it available to nearly everyone. Many people who never skated before tried out the sport and found it to be great and enjoyable exercise.

Roller-skating has its origins in ice skating. The first roller skates were usually copied from various models of ice skates featuring from two to six wheels attached to a wooden "plate" and arranged in an inline fashion to imitate ice "blades." This design actually is similar to today's inline skates, but one could only skate in a straight line. In 1863, J.L. Plimpton of Massachusetts revolutionized the skating world by inventing the "rocking action" skate. It was the first model of a roller skate that could be steered or guided and started the first roller-skating craze around the United States and the entire world. Due to this design, the skater was able to maneuver freely and perform moves similar to those of ice skating.

Skates back in the 1940s were different than they are now. The original roller skates had wooden wheels and the floors at the rinks were wooden, so it was easier to slide or break a wheel. Today's wheels are made of polyurethane, which originally became popular in the 1960s. Toe-stops were perfected in the 1940s and commercially produced in the 1950s.

Today's jamskaters use toe plugs to stop their movement, allowing them to do more difficult tricks and maneuvers.

Back in the 1940s, there were strap-on skates, and when you came to the arena, skate boys would put the skates on your shoes with clampers. Clamp-on roller skates were invented in 1863 by a Massachusetts inventor, E.H. Barney, and were perfected in the 1890s. Clamp-on skates have a two-piece adjustable-length roller-skate plate that enables a single pair of skates to fit people with varying shoe sizes. The clamp-on type of roller skate fits over your shoe and is fastened to your shoe's soles by using a skate key. The use of the sliding front and rear plates to adjust to the growth of a child's foot continued into the 1960s. While professional skaters of that era used "shoe skates," the general public used clamp-on skates until the 1950s.

In the 1940s, if you were wealthy enough to have your own skates, you would have a traditional boot skate. In general, men wore black skates, and women wore white skates. Back then, professional-grade skates cost between $17 and $20. Today, professional-grade skates cost between $600 and $700. Top competitors have their skates custom made and molded to fit their feet to suit their equipment preferences. These custom-made skates can cost well over $1,500.

Today's inline skates are similar to the first roller skates and are affixed to an assembly called the frame rather than a plate like traditional skates. Since 1990, inline skates have been improved, and roller skaters are discovering the advantages of inline skates, especially the increased speed. Both roller speed and hockey disciplines now feature inline skates almost exclusively for national and international competition.

There are two main types of skating: artistic skating and roller speed skating. Both artistic skating and roller speed skating were performed at the Perth Amboy Arena. Artistic roller skating includes three types of skating: figure, freestyle and skate dancing.

Figure skating is made up of set, formalized movements and steps. Freestyle skating, which originated from figure skating, incorporates routines individual to each roller skater or skating couple. Both figure and freestyle skating were performed together during competition until 1949. The early development of figure skating on roller skates came from ice skaters. Roller skaters eventually created an itinerary of more than forty figures of jumps, turns and spins. As time went by, freestyle roller skaters began adapting movements from ice skaters in the 1930s and 1940s. Roller skaters began creating their own movements. During the 1940s, after completing the required figure-skating movements during competition, a roller skater could then perform his or her own fancy tricks to reveal his or her skill as a skater. In 1949, freestyle separated from figures, resulting in its own competition. Freestyle skating involves interpreting the tempo and mood of the music during the routine, and each skater is judged by his or her speed, height of jumps, sureness of spins and connective footwork.

Dance roller skating began in the nineteenth century. Jackson Haines, an American ballet teacher and ice figure skater living in Vienna, introduced skate dancing to the United States. At first it only mimicked ballroom dancing, and then as time went on, other dances were introduced. In 1939, roller skate dance became a competitive sport, and soon after, many dances were created especially for roller skaters.

The America on Wheels Arena hosted competitions including New Jersey state competitions, national competitions and various other invitational meets in such categories as novice figures, school figures and freestyle events. Both men and women competed. Daniel Yovanovich, born in 1921, the son of Serbian immigrants and a longtime skater, remembers fondly the skating rink in Perth Amboy. He always enjoyed skating because it's great exercise and "in skating you can do your thing." Daniel and his two brothers, Alex and Robert, all competed in the Perth Amboy roller rink. They also competed with George Durnye and his brother, John. John Durnye presently owns the South Amboy Arena part of the Rollermagic Rinks chain. John met his wife, Marie, at the Perth Amboy Arena. John and Marie competed together in dance, and John competed in novice freestyle. Daniel competed in state, national and America on Wheels competitions in the novice freestyle events. Daniel also competed in dance with partner Rosemarie Brantley. Back then, only couples competed in dance since there were no single dance categories like there are today where a man or woman would compete on his or her own. Daniel won two medals, both for novice freestyle: one for a state competition and one for an America on Wheels competition. The America on Wheels rinks held competitions between rinks, and Daniel competed in some of those contests and won a medal for novice freestyle.

The owner of the America on Wheels chain of roller rinks was Bill Schmitz, who owned eight roller rinks by the 1940s, an empire he built starting in 1934 with a pint-sized forty- by eighty-foot skating rink in Closter, New Jersey, and just $100 in cash. Defying the odds and everything said against him that it could not be done, Schmitz's roller rinks grew as he opened one in Palisades Park in 1935; in Paterson, New Jersey, in 1936; and, in the same year, rinks in Lake Hopatcong and White Plains, New Jersey (an upstairs loft). Then he opened a rink in Long Branch, New Jersey, and in the same year (1938) a rink in Passaic, New Jersey, and then one in Mountain View on Route 23. Christmas Day 1939 was the opening of the huge arena in Perth Amboy. Later in 1940, a rink was opened in the Casino in Asbury Park, New Jersey, and then Schmitz opened the Capitol Arena in Trenton, New Jersey. In 1940, America on Wheels opened up the big Boulevard Arena in Bayonne, New Jersey. Later in 1940, Schmitz opened the Mount Vernon Arena. In 1941 came the Twin City Arena, flagship of the outfit, and then the St. Nicholas Arena in New York City.[95]

Dance skating competitions were when a man and woman would dance together on roller skates and compete against other couples. There were also club competitions, where the clubs would come dressed alike in uniforms. For example, they would wear white pants and red shirts with a logo on the back. There were prizes for who had the best outfits or which club brought the most skaters. Both clubs and individuals would come from all around the tri-state area just to skate in Perth Amboy. The prizes were trophies, plaques, medals or bowls. They were strictly amateur, and no money was awarded for prizes. Perth Amboy had its own clubs, such as the Top Hatters, Three Star Rollers and the Lucky Rollers. The Lucky Rollers won over twelve trophies from 1938 through 1941. Other roller-skating clubs included the All American Rollers from Port Reading, the U.S. Rollers and Moonlight Rollers from Plainfield, the Villa Drill Team from Broadway, the Dreamland Skating Club from Newark and the American Rollers, Inc. from Irvington, New Jersey. The arena also hosted numerous award ceremonies to honor its skaters. These ceremonies were as well attended as the rink's famous parties.

Daniel Yovanovich recalls many parties and competitions in the Perth Amboy rink. The parties included such themes as "Sweethearts

The Top Hatters, one of many Perth Amboy skating clubs that won numerous trophies in their time. *Courtesy of Chester Freid.*

Parties" for Valentine's Day or themes for other respective holidays such as Christmas, Halloween, the Fourth of July and many other special occasions. These parties included games, prizes and door prizes.

Daniel still skates twice a week. "I started skating in 1939 and started competing in 1942." He met his wife, Theresa, in high school but started dating her when she and her sister used to skate at the America on Wheels Perth Amboy Arena. Some of Daniel's fond memories of the arena included trios. Sometimes there were trios that consisted of two men and one woman, or there would be one man and two women. The trio would skate as fast as they could around the rink. "Dust would come up like someone was mixing cement," Yovanovich fondly remembers.

Back in the 1940s, there was a rule that women's skirts had to be no more than four inches above the knee. One of the two guards at the door checked the length of each woman's skirt to make sure it was long enough. Unless there was a party, in which case, of course, anything goes!

Above: The Lucky Rollers, another Perth Amboy skating club. *Courtesy of Chester Freid.*

Left: Joseph Pop Haas, the doorman at the America on Wheels Perth Amboy Arena. *Courtesy of Chester Freid.*

During the 1940s at the height of World War II, you were considered well off if you owned your own car. Despite this, the arena's parking lot was filled to the brim every night. Yovanovich fondly remembers, "On the holidays there were parties and thousands came. Nowadays everyone is home for the holidays and everything is closed. Back then everywhere was open on the holidays and you went to a party." These parties were so popular that the arena was packed with skaters from all over New Jersey, New York and neighboring states. It was not uncommon for two thousand people to attend one of America on Wheel's skating parties. They were so crowded and so full of skaters that if a trio fell down, there would be a pile of people before the guards got to them. Clubs, groups and people who simply loved skating enjoyed themselves so much that memories of these magnificent parties bring smiles to the faces of those individuals who remember the good times they once had at the Perth Amboy Arena.

According to longtime Perth Amboy resident Ila Miller, at one time Perth Amboy boasted several skating arenas. There was one located on New Brunswick Avenue that was open for a short period of time. It closed due to competition from the America on Wheels Arena.

The America on Wheels Perth Amboy Arena brought people from the entire tri-state area to Perth Amboy. The Tottenville Ferry, complete with its own monkey grinder, brought many patrons to Perth Amboy for skating at the rink from Staten Island and other parts of New York. These people patronized the town, its shops, restaurants, stores, theaters and everything else it had to offer, including its famous waterfront. Perth Amboy had a lot to offer the people back in the 1930s and 1940s, and much of this business and patronage was due to people coming for the sole reason of roller skating. People would make a day of it—come into town, shop, eat, go see a movie or show and then go skate. These shops, restaurants, hotels, theaters and everything else Perth Amboy had to offer slowly faded away after the rink closed in 1949, an event that trickled down into the 1960s and 1970s and still today has yet to recapture the grandeur that this city once had. Today, aside from a few bright spots such as Perth Amboy's famous waterfront, the newly built YMCA and some restaurants, everyone in Perth Amboy goes elsewhere for their entertainment. It is interesting to think that Perth Amboy once had a roller rink so large and grand that everyone around came to Perth Amboy just to skate.

The America on Wheels Skating Arena in Perth Amboy closed in 1949 when its ten-year lease expired. Philip-Carey bought the lease and converted the rink to a factory that manufactured tar, tarpaper for roofing and asbestos shingles on the site in the 1950s. Philip-Carey had offered more money than the America on Wheels company, and the owners of the building decided that short-term profits of a factory were more important than the long-term profits of skating. They viewed skating as a passing fad and thought that the employment of a few hundred individuals was more important than skating.

The company Celotex, which also manufactured tar, tarpaper and asbestos shingles, eventually bought out Philip-Carey. The Celotex company filed for bankruptcy in 1998 and eventually closed all its sites, including the one in Perth Amboy in 2002. The building was demolished. The property is presently undeveloped, and vegetation has grown over the area, although the remains of the foundation of the building are still visible to this day. It is wasting away as unused and undeveloped land and is considered contaminated due to the chemicals used by the factories that once occupied the area.

Skating has changed over the years but still remains a popular activity. Inline skates have replaced quads for the most part. When asked what longtime skater Daniel Yovanovich thought of today's inline skates, he simply stated, "You can go very, very fast in them—much faster than on quads."

Many people of all ages still skate daily despite the mentality of the Perth Amboy business owners of the late 1940s that forced the closing of the rink. Today, Perth Amboy is graced with a local figure who is featured on YouTube. He is a man of sixty-plus years of age, which does not show in his dancing moves. You may have seen him dancing and skating in the street to music. He is called the "Dancing Perth Amboy Roller Skating Man" or simply the "Skating Man" or the "Dancing Man." If you are lucky enough to see him dance, you are graced with his vitality. He is featured on YouTube for the world to see and enjoy his skate dancing moves, and indeed, he can move and move well.

One must stop and think what Perth Amboy could have been had the arena never closed. The parties and the clanking of the wooden roller skates are all just fond memories to those who remember the glory days of the America on Wheels Arena and the grandeur it once brought to Perth Amboy. One must still ponder what could have been...

Chapter 11

A STROLL DOWN SMITH STREET

1930s–1980s

Filled with energy and bustling with activity and crowded streets, downtown Perth Amboy was the place to be from the 1940s through the 1960s. Longtime residents remember the streets as being "clean and safe," states Perth Amboy–born Eleanor Kataryniak. Perth Amboy's stores were filled to capacity with patrons who came from all over New Jersey and New York. A newcomer to Perth Amboy can easily note that the city is one of contrasts that grew out of early life in the town. Perth Amboy had grown in the nineteenth and twentieth centuries and became a business center, which included industrial factories, shops and eight theaters. The downtown streets and shops were filled with pedestrians every Monday through Friday. Perth Amboy featured department stores, specialty shops, beauty parlors and restaurants. There were stores in Perth Amboy for all of your needs. "It was pleasant to shop. Anything you ever wanted you could probably find. If it was a special occasion and you couldn't find the item and you had a rapport with the store, the salesperson would help you get it. It was good-quality stuff," Kataryniak states.

Perth Amboy native Reggie Navarro states, "Downtown was the place to shop. You had some good stores." Lifelong Perth Amboy resident Carolyn Maxwell remembers that in the summertime there were

Born in Perth Amboy, Eleanor Kataryniak remembers old Smith Street like it was yesterday. *Photo by the author.*

Born in Perth Amboy, Reggie Navarro owns the Courthouse Inn on Fayette Street. He has very fond memories of downtown Perth Amboy. *Photo by the author.*

midnight sales just before school. "We would go shopping, then go home for dinner, then go back and do some more shopping." "You would find families with children shopping," Kataryniak states.

Reynolds Department store, a local favorite, featured pneumatic tubes in which money was exchanged. Lifelong Perth Amboy resident Barbara Stack remembers Reynolds: "My grandmother, Ellen Stack, worked in Reynolds. I used to go visit her. The store had an elevator. I remember the pneumatic tubes. It was a novelty. You would give your money with the bill to the saleslady.

Lifelong Perth Amboy resident Carolyn Maxwell remembers the good times in the glory days of Amboy. *Photo by Paul W. Wang.*

She would put the bill along with the money into the tube. It would come back with your change." Lifelong Perth Amboy resident Joan Zaleski remembers, "The pneumatic tubes used to amaze me." The pneumatic tubes would fascinate the children who visited the store. Lifelong Perth Amboy resident Jack M. Dudas remembers the elevator in Reynolds: "Mr. Reynolds's portrait was hung above the elevator." Dudas's maternal grandmother, Gertrude Keating, used to take him uptown. "The prices were great," Dudas states.

Perth Amboy's five-and-dime stores included such businesses as Woolworth's, S.S. Kresge's, H.L. Green, W.T. Grant and McCrory's. At 84–86 Smith Street was Woolworth's. The five-and-dime store was a prelude to the dollar store of today, and Woolworth's boasted that no items were more than ten cents each. Palms, dapper clerks, oiled wooden floors and walnut merchandise display tables all added to the ambience.

Tony Massopust states that he got his first chipped beef on toast at Woolworth's lunch counter. Woolworth's had a great toy department. Dudas states, "During the 100th anniversary of the Civil War, I would buy a bag of soldiers for ninety-nine cents at Woolworth's." Navarro states, "Woolworth's had sundae specials. There were balloons there. If you popped the right balloon, you could win a free sundae or one at a discounted price."

Lifelong resident of Perth Amboy Marcella Massopust's favorite stores were Reynolds and Woolworth's. She also remembers fondly Schindel's Clothing store located at 97–105 Smith Street, which featured lower-priced clothing. She also loved Finks department store, which was owned and operated in Perth Amboy for years. "Finks had dishes, glassware and pots, and people loved it. We used to shop on Friday. The stores were open until 6:00 p.m. on weekdays, 10:00 p.m. on Friday and 6:00 p.m. on Saturday." Friday night was shopping night for many of the people of Perth Amboy. Since there were blue laws from the 1930s up until the

My mother, Marcella Massopust, a lifelong resident of Perth Amboy. She remembers the downtown area with fondness. *Photo by the author.*

1980s, many people window-shopped on Sundays, adding to their wish lists for the following week as they passed many of the store windows.

Anne Rothlein, who grew up and lived in Perth Amboy for many years, remembers fondly Lerners and Wilks, which were nice for women's clothes. Stack remembers that you could just walk from store to store and shop. "As a little girl, my mother took me downtown, and we stopped and walked everywhere. Every store was different. My favorite store was the Surprise shop. It had children's clothes and everything."

Kataryniak loved S. Fine. "It had quality-style clothing—some better than in New York stores. People would come from Staten Island to come to that store. The salespeople were very nice and pleasant."

Other stores that were fondly remembered were Shirley Spiegels, May's Dress Store, Pride 'n Joy (a children's store), the Army-Navy Store, Paramount, Martin Shapiro, Jerry Price and Jag's Sporting Goods. Youth Fashion sold infant and children's clothing, communion dresses and suits for girls and boys up to ten years old. Levine's was a sporting goods store. Fishkin's was on Madison Avenue and sold sporting goods and toys, as well as photography supplies, hunting supplies and fishing supplies. Park Lynn, St. Leifer and Alexander's sold men's clothes. Sears was on Hobart Street. A.S. & Beck was on the corner of Hobart and Smith Streets and sold shoes. Other shoe stores in Perth Amboy were Thom McCann, Boston, Allyn's, Goldsmith's, Kolber Slautkas, Slobodian's, National Shoes and Cherensky's. Rothlein remembers that Slobodian's had an X-ray machine: "After you bought your shoes, you had an X-ray taken of your foot to see how your foot fit in your shoes." Kataryniak loved Boston Shoes: "The service was excellent. If you wanted something for a special occasion, they would order it for you. Quality leather shoes were sold. I still have a few pairs." Boston Shoes also featured an X-ray machine. It had shoes for women, men and children. Cherensky's made shoes if you had special needs. American Shoe repaired shoes and leather goods. "The Tarantino family owned the business. You could have your shoes repaired while you waited. You were treated as a family member," Kataryniak remembers.

Gimpleman's sold paint, wallpaper and blinds. Spevacks sold blinds and all types of window treatments. King's Men Shop sold hundreds of ties, shirts and jackets. Lee Luggage was on the lower part of Smith Street. Fabric Center offered materials for those who made their own

Briegs the Tailor made men's suits. Located on Smith Street, it was one of many businesses patronized by the town. *Courtesy of Stephen Michael Dudash.*

clothing. Wahrendorf's and Clark the Florist were both florists. Mae Moon sold uniforms and older women's dresses. Littman's, Robert's and Kreilsheiner's sold jewelry. Golden Jewelers was above Penn Loan. Briegs the Tailor made custom suits for men. Albert Leon Furniture had quality pieces that people came from all around to buy. Polonia Furniture on State Street also had top-quality solid wood furniture.

Sam Fox rented tuxedos. Dublin Plumbing & Supply sold plumbing supplies, and Charles Fagan Hardware Company sold hardware. Majestic Lanes, on the corner of Madison Avenue and Smith Street (where Fink Plaza is now), offered bowling to local patrons. Panter Motors sold Pontiac products. There were also Van Sickles and Polkowitz Motors. There was a furrier in town called Fox the Furrier.

Carolyn Maxwell remembers Thom McCann, Lerners, Paramount, Robert Hall and Reynolds: "Every fall I would go to Thom McCann and get my new penny loafers, and I would put a penny in each shoe." Robert Hall (now the site of Sipo's Bakery) featured sensible clothing. It was often packed with patrons. Dobb's Millinery sold women's hats, tiaras, veils and gloves for weddings. Bee Bee's Millinery sold hats and hosiery. Ann's was a children's shop that sold clothing for ages infant to fourteen years. Many children were brought home from Perth Amboy General Hospital in clothing from Ann's. May's Dress Shop sold women's clothing, while Archie Jacobson's sold men's clothes.

During the 1970s and up to the mid-1980s, Mickey Finn's offered prime brand names of clothing at bargain prices. When the store closed in the late 1980s, it was eventually replaced by Margarita's thrift shop, which sells secondhand clothing and other bargain items.

There was also Mechanics Toy Store, which featured juvenile furniture, bicycles and toys for all ages. "I used to buy my toy soldiers in Mechanics," Tony Massopust states. Dudas remembers Mechanics as well: "Mechanics was great. If he [the owner] didn't have what you wanted, he would order it for you."

Dudas also remembers going with Fred Fishkin every Friday when in high school during the 1960s to buy model and paint supplies and records at Fishkin's. "We both had tropical fish, so we went for supplies on Fridays to Joe's Pet Shop. You could also buy records at Stan Morris'." Navarro states, "Fishkin's had bicycles, remote-controlled model planes—it had everything."

Many longtime residents remember food shopping in Perth Amboy. Supermarkets in Amboy included the A&P located on Maple Street where C-Town is presently located. Acme Market, often mentioned in *Looney Tunes Cartoons* as a place where you can buy anything, was located on Maple Street near the A&P. Foodtown served many residents when it moved into the old Strand Theater building. Those who shopped at Foodtown could see the structure where the screen once was. Presently, Rite Aid stands on this site in a new building constructed in the late 1990s.

Foodland used to be Auction Hall next to Hotel Central. At one time, Amboy and Rust Company was located in the building. There were many mom and pop stores all over town. Barbara Stack remembers, "There was a mom and pop store across the street from my house on High Street. I remember when frozen food came out, the fish sticks and all the frozen food were in one case."

There also was Young's Meat Market in between McClellan and Maple Streets. Handerhan's and Rasmunsen's were fish markets. During the 1950s, there was also home delivery by Lambrecht Foods.

Joan Zaleski, my aunt (my mother's sister), a lifelong resident of Perth Amboy. She has many fond memories of the town. *Photo by the author.*

During the late 1950s and early '60s, there was a knife sharpener who had a wheel and walked up and down the streets. He would yell, "Knives!" All the women would come out, and he would sharpen their knives for a fee. There also was a shoeshine man who yelled, "Shine!" Anyone needing a shine came out.

Perth Amboy was filled with restaurants. Massopust remembers fondly, "I loved Coney Island hot dogs." Zaleski speaks fondly of the Nancy Lee Bakery: "We used to buy birthday cakes there."

On top of Woolworth's was an elegant Chinese restaurant upstairs featuring dark booths with white tablecloths. Kataryniak remembers it as her favorite restaurant as a child.

Kataryniak and Zaleski remember Parnes Bakery and Corner Bake Shop on New Brunswick Avenue. The bakery was open seven days a week. It had a large variety of pastries, cakes, cookies and bread. "At 5:00 p.m., you could get fresh homemade breakfast buns," Kataryniak states. "When they made fresh rolls, you could smell them all over Perth Amboy," Zaleski adds.

Kataryniak remembers Boston Ice Cream Parlor, which also sold candy. There also were Loft's Candy, Fanny Farmer and the Amboy Candy Kitchen. The Majestic Pharmacy was at Maple and Smith Streets.

"I used to go the Crystal with all of my school friends," Zaleski states. Stack remembers, "Both Coney Island and the Crystal had Coney Island hot dogs. I used to go to both restaurants. I also used to go to Pamel's and Burlfein's. Burlfein's was across the street from the high school. Lido Gardens in the Packer House had great food. I also loved Sciortino's Pizza." Longtime resident of Perth Amboy Faith Hernandez states, "I loved Coney Island hot dogs and Hungarian goulash."

"I used to go to Politie's on Madison Avenue with my mother," Massopust remembers. Madison Pine was Kataryniak's favorite restaurant as an adult. "You would see anyone from Perth Amboy in there."

The Texas Lunch on Smith Street was another popular attraction. It is now the office of Dr. Elaine Mariolis, DPM.

Jack M. Dudas remembers the Italian restaurant Mandica's, which had two locations in Perth Amboy until the business was moved to Woodbridge. "I used to love their ravioli."

At one time, Perth Amboy hosted eight theaters: the Strand, Crescent, Proctor's, Ditmas, Roky, Majestic, Royal and Bijou. The theaters would give out dishes as an incentive to go to the movies. Thursday night was dish night at the Majestic. People wanted the entire set, so they would come back every week to the movie theater.

Marcella Massopust remembers the Roky as her favorite theater. "It was a kids' theater. We used to go to the serials every Saturday morning. Then we would go to Boston Ice Cream Parlor for a banana split. The Majestic was classier; I saw *Snow White* at the Majestic."

Zaleski remembers the Crescent and the Roky: "As a child, my favorite theater was the Roky. I loved the serials." The Roky was called the Garlic House because the men who worked there smelled of garlic on their breath. Often a box of Duz soap with dish towels in it was given to the patrons.

Rothlein's favorite theater was the Majestic. She saw many movies in that theater. Stack enjoyed the Strand, the Majestic and the Royal: "I saw *Gone with the Wind* and a bunch of movies. They used to have double features. You saw the newsreels at the movie theater. Back then, television was new and most people didn't have one. One of our neighbors had a television. We would watch it there." Zaleski fondly remembers the theater as well: "When *The Robe* came out, there were lines and lines of people." Tony Massopust remembers, "I used to see live vaudeville at the Majestic every Tuesday and Thursday." Dudas remembers the Majestic and the Royal: "I liked the Majestic better because it was bigger and had better movies." Navarro loved the Majestic: "There was a giant ball in the lobby. You had to guess how many balls were in it. If you did, you won something." There was a spiral staircase going up to the balcony. It was a favorite for couples.

Tony Massopust remembers, "The Ditmas was across the street from the high school." Kataryniak loved the Ditmas: "It ran the first-run good movies."

Carolyn Maxwell remembers the Majestic and the Royal: "I saw *Jason and the Argonauts* with my sister. We were the only teenagers there. The rest was little kids in the theater. I saw *Alien* at the Royal. There were a lot of little kids in the front row. When the alien popped out of the guy's stomach, all the kids in the front row screamed and ran in the back."

In the 1950s, downtown Perth Amboy was the place to be. "Cruise night" was every Friday night as cars drove up and down Smith Street with pride. Marcella Massopust stated, "I went with friends of mine who had cars. It was fun!" Zaleski remembers fondly, "We called it 'bugging the stem.'" Tony Massopust remembers, "They would gas up in King High Garage and ride up High Street and down Smith Street, then gas up in King High and go ride up again around City Hall Circle up Smith Street and down Silzer Street." "Traffic was bumper to bumper," Stack states. "I used to love to cruise on down Smith Street on Friday night," Dudas remembers fondly. "It was nice, harmless fun," Maxwell comments. "We had a lot of fun," Hernandez states.

Cruise night ended in the early 1970s when the local police decided it was a public nuisance and banned it, much to the dismay of local businesses that benefited from "bugging the stem" traffic. The chief of police barricaded Smith Street so no traffic could go up or down the street. He did not like the idea of cruising. Many local establishments felt this hurt their business. Cruise night is now just fond memories for many people.

Parades abounded in the 1950s for almost every occasion. Marcella Massopust remembers the Army-Navy parade for Army-Navy Day. She also remembers that Perth Amboy High School would have a

A parade possibly for Labor Day in September 1940. The Lion's Club Drum and Bugle Corps march up Smith Street in front of the Strand Theater. Note the Hotel Packer in the background. *Courtesy of the Perth Amboy Free Public Library.*

parade every Saturday if it won the football game. Everyone marched out of Water's Stadium up Eagle Avenue, down Amboy Avenue, down New Brunswick Avenue, down Smith Street and down State Street to Amboy High School. They then sang the alma mater on the lawn of the Halls of Ivy.

Stack remembers the Easter Parade down the waterfront as a child: "My cousin and her family won one year as a family." For Memorial Day, there were parades with veterans of many wars and also local firemen who were honored. These veterans included those of the Spanish American War (1898), World War I and World War II and, later, the Korean War. The Gold Star Mothers (mothers of servicemen who lost their lives during wartime) marched or were driven in the parade. The Sea Scouts who trained at the armory also marched. Tanks and other military vehicles graced the streets. On Patriot's Day, military vehicles

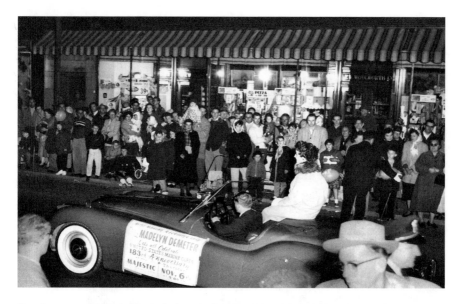

Parades were popular in Perth Amboy during the 1950s. Many honored the U.S. military. This parade was circa 1957. Pictured is Madelyn Demeter, marine recruiter. *Courtesy of the Perth Amboy Free Public Library.*

rode up Perth Amboy's streets. The tanks were so heavy that they damaged the pavement.

Dudas remembers the Halloween parades. The art classes of Perth Amboy High School art teacher Anne Massopust (my paternal grandmother) and Ida Dressler used to paint the windows for Halloween downtown. Festive scenes of goblins and ghouls would delight patrons throughout Halloween. The streets were also always decorated for Christmas. Navarro states, "The Salvation Army used to play trumpets for Christmas. People were always singing carols."

One of the big events was the high school prom. Perth Amboy High School (now McGinnis School) held the proms in the gymnasium. The gym was decorated with streamers and confetti. "The theme of one of the proms was 'stars fell on Alabama.' They decorated the gym with stars made of crepe paper hanging from the ceiling," Zaleski remembers.

Stack remembers going to New York by train from Perth Amboy to go to the Broadway shows. "I saw *The Andersonville Trial* with William Shatner and George C. Scott. I saw *Peter Pan* (the movie) in Radio City Music Hall."

Maxwell remembers a bus terminal ticket agency owned by New Jersey Transit on Smith and Oak Street: "I used to go on bus trips to Connecticut and other places." It is now the Primavera Bakery.

On the corner of McClellan Street and Smith Street was Keene's Boys' Club, which mainly offered recreational activities for young boys. On Fridays and Saturdays, there were dances there. Hernandez remembers going there with her brother Noel Palazzo. St. Mary's also featured a Friday night dance in its high school gym.

Mizerak's Pool Club was on Madison Avenue. Hernandez remembers watching the late pool champion Steve Mizerak play pool there.

Perth Amboy had its share of fires and disasters. People remember when Schindel's burned down. Other prominent fires were the Roth Furniture fire, Chevron Oil fire and Hurley Lumberyard fire on William Street. And anyone who was there never forgets the Packer Hotel fire. One of the more prominent buildings, the Packer Hotel stood tall on Smith Street with one hundred rooms and forty-eight baths. It housed Lido Gardens, which many Perth Amboy residents believed had the best Chinese food in town. The Packer Hotel fire started on the cold winter night of March 17, 1969. A mattress caught fire at the hotel, most likely due to residents smoking in bed. The residents attempted to put out the fire themselves; after they believed the fire was out, they dragged the mattress through the hallways, not realizing it was still smoldering. A hot amber became embedded in the carpeting that lined the halls, and several hours later, the carpeting caught fire. That fire spread throughout the building, claimed many lives and completely destroyed the building. During the 1970s, the United Auto Workers (UAW) built a senior housing facility on the site. Some of the residents claim the building is haunted and they hear strange noises in the middle of the night.

In 1969, Rogers Clothes burned down, along with Richard's Bookstore. Another famous fire was the Cableworks fire on July 9, 1980, which lasted for nine days. The fire was believed to be caused by a spark near cleaning solvents. The Cableworks was completely destroyed, and the site is now a vacant lot. Dudas remembers just having joined the volunteer fire department when he got into the action.

Another famous disaster is the South Amboy Munitions explosion, which occurred on May 19, 1950. A cloud of smoke could be seen over South Amboy. "At 7:36 p.m. an estimated 150 tons of military

On July 9, 1980, tragedy struck Perth Amboy with the Cableworks fire, also known as the Duane Marine Fire. Many businesses were lost due to the fire that lasted for nine days. This photo shows Jack M. Dudas on the ladder truck. *Courtesy of Jack M. Dudas, Esq.*

explosives and gelatin dynamite exploded at a pier at the base of Rosewell Street. Twenty-six longshoremen and five barge captains were killed, though only the remains of a few were ever recovered."[96] Stack remembers, "I was five years old. I went outside and saw the smoke. My cousin Donna Stack, who was also five years old at the time, lived at 263 McClellan Street. She had just gotten up from where she was sitting near the window to do something when the explosion happened. The windows blew outward. Her family's house had twenty-two windows blown out. The curtains in the living room windows wound up in the trees on McClellan Street in front of her house. Her family would find glass in their coat pockets months later." She was not the only one; Smith Street had windows blown out, as did many buildings in Perth Amboy. Kataryniak remembers, "The windows of A.S. & Beck were all blown out." Stack stated that Pam Mullen—whose father, Eugene, owned Mullen's Funeral Home at 196 Market Street on the corner of Market and McClellan Street—said, "You couldn't cross the street in Perth Amboy because of all the cars on the street coming into Perth Amboy, coming to see what had happened."

One last notable stop in Perth Amboy was Seaman's Pharmacy, a landmark until the day it closed. It was relocated twice. Its first location was on High Street, where its owners helped during the Great Depression by serving soup to the needy. That building on High Street is now the office of a dentist, Dr. Peter L. DeSciscio. In the mid-1930s, Seaman's Pharmacy moved to 82 Smith Street, where it remained until it closed its doors on November 19, 1998. Many local residents patronized the pharmacy, which had an old-fashioned soda fountain, counter and booths and tin walls and ceilings that gave the shop character. Even to the day it closed, Seaman's had a sit-down phone booth that still was operational. Seaman's Pharmacy held many happy memories for those who worked and patronized the store, whether it was for coffee, lunch or simply to pick up their prescriptions. Local residents such as famed actor Charlie White, local artist Vince Alba and lawyer Jack M. Dudas often frequented the establishment. Rothlein remembers going to Seaman's:

One of the many notable stops on Smith Street, Seaman's Pharmacy was famous for its fountain, wooden phone booth and great lunch counter. Many professionals came to Seaman's to socialize. Pictured on the last day Seaman's was open, November 19, 1998, is local actor Charles White and Seaman's owner James Hardiman serving the last cup of coffee. *Courtesy of Barbara Booz.*

"Every Sunday I had a vanilla ice cream sundae with their famous butterscotch sauce. It was so good." Hernandez would get her sundaes on Saturday evenings.

As time went on in the 1980s, many factories closed their doors in Perth Amboy as industry left town to go elsewhere. During the 1970s and 1980s, the malls came to Edison and Woodbridge, drawing business out of town. Many stores left Perth Amboy, and the town's golden age ended. Presently, the majority of businesses in town are nail salons, buzz shops, ninety-nine-cent stores and a smattering of restaurants. Many of these businesses are transient and do not stay long. There are businesses that have remained in the city for many years, such as Fertigs and Alvarez Cigars. Many of these businesses are family owned and have passed from generation to generation and remain the exception to the rule of the many transient businesses that populate our town. The face of Smith Street has changed over the years and the future of stores and businesses in Perth Amboy remains to be seen, but its history will remain in the hearts of many forever.

Chapter 12

THE PERTH AMBOY HIGH SCHOOL BASKETBALL TEAM WINS THE STATE CHAMPIONSHIP

March 30, 1968

It took fifty years, but Perth Amboy finally made it to the state championships in the Interschool System Association Basketball Tournament. It was the third time that Perth Amboy had made it through the semifinals in modern-day basketball. In 1968, the Perth Amboy High School basketball team had twenty-four wins with one loss. (The only loss was to South River.) Six times they scored more than 100 points in a game that season. Teamwork, camaraderie, school spirit—these all describe the 1968 Perth Amboy High School basketball team. The teammates worked together and clicked like clockwork to achieve their goals. Led by future NBA star forward Brian Taylor, the Perth Amboy Panthers were heading to the state championships against rival Neptune's Scarlet Fliers in Atlantic City, New Jersey. Coach Bill Buglovsky stated, as quoted in the *Perth Amboy Evening News*, "It is a team that is unmatched for desire and determination…it wants that one big title."[97]

There were four tournament preliminary games against Plainfield, Linden, Thomas Jefferson and Hackensack. Group IV consisted of the largest schools in the state. "Mission impossible became a reality Saturday night when the scrappy Panthers doomed to almost certain defeat with 2:46 left in the game pulled off a dramatic if not unbelievable 64–61 triumph over Hackensack at Convention Hall."[98]

Group four semifinals, 1968, Perth Amboy versus Linden at Rutgers Gym on College Avenue. *Photo by Bob Ned.*

The team then faced Neptune in the Atlantic City Convention Center. The price was three dollars per ticket. The tournament was a two-day, seven-game NJSIAA (New Jersey State Interscholastic Athletic Association) basketball finals.

The Perth Amboy Panthers' starting lineup was Noel Lugo at guard, Harold Brown at guard, Wayne Pennyfeather at forward, Pete Marvookas at center and, of course, the star, Brian Taylor, at forward. (Taylor would play guard, center or forward as the occasion demanded.) Taylor was six and a half feet and 165 pounds and became the fourth player in Perth Amboy High School history to pass the 1,000-point mark in 1968. At practice the week before, Brown suffered a concussion so he was unable to play. He was replaced by substitute guard Andy Seaman.

Everyone was excited; almost all of Perth Amboy was in attendance. The actual paid attendance was 23,314 patrons on that Saturday, March 30, 1968. As the game began, Taylor was challenged by Neptune's star,

Perth Amboy Panthers versus Hackensack Comets. *Photo by Bob Ned.*

Kenny O'Donnell. O'Donnell matched Taylor shot for shot. The game was close all night long. Each team had the lead at one time or another. Perth Amboy would play man-to-man defense, while Neptune oscillated between man-to-man and zone defense. The crowd was on pins and needles and roared, "We're No. 1!" for Perth Amboy. Head cheerleader Kathy Novak stirred the crowd while Brenda Maxwell did her famous Russian splits.

Neptune did everything to try to stop Taylor. They double-teamed him to no avail. The Panthers were ahead for the first three periods, but then Neptune got 8 straight points and took the lead 69–64. Taylor and Marvookas were able to regain the lead—until the last seventy-three seconds. The score was 70–70, and Neptune had the ball. O'Donnell dribbled until there were nine seconds on the clock, and then he attempted to make his shot. Almost everyone had their heads down. But then a miracle happened—he missed! Taylor grabbed the ball and dribbled

Above: Perth Amboy Panthers versus Neptune Scarlet Fliers. The tournament took place in the Atlantic City Convention Center. *Photo by Bob Ned.*

Left: Perth Amboy Panthers versus Neptune Scarlet Fliers, 1968 basketball championship. *Photo by Bob Ned.*

Perth Amboy Panthers versus Neptune Scarlet Fliers, 1968 basketball championship. *Photo by Bob Ned.*

down the court. He was fouled down court with two seconds left on the clock. Tried and true, Taylor made his foul shots, putting Amboy in the lead. Perth Amboy won!

The 1968 basketball team was an example of winners. No one took all the credit. They were a team, and despite being underdogs, they went on to victory in the first ever state basketball championship in Perth Amboy history. "Despite their superior height advantage, Neptune was beaten off the boards."[99] the *Perth Amboy Evening News* stated. The team was honored with a party down on Perth Amboy's waterfront, where the city celebrated the team's victory.

Neptune's Kenny O'Donnell would eventually be drafted to play minor-league baseball (shortstop) for the Kansas City Royals. Brian Taylor graduated from Princeton University and then was drafted by the Seattle Supersonics in the second round of the 1972 NBA draft. However, Taylor began his career in the American Basketball Association playing for the New York Nets. He was the 1972 ABA Rookie of the Year (guard) for the Nets. He led the Nets to a league title in 1976. When the ABA and NBA merged, Taylor asked to be traded. He was dealt to the Kansas City Kings, where he spent one year. He continued his basketball career playing for the Denver Nuggets and San Diego Clippers.

Brian Taylor scored a total of 2,495 points while at Perth Amboy High School. In 1989, he was inducted into the Perth Amboy Hall of Fame along with his brother, Bruce Taylor, who played for the San Francisco 49ers. Brian Taylor is presently a high school principal in Los Angeles.

In 2010, local resident Al Jackson made a documentary on the 1968 basketball team, and the members had a reunion.

Today when asked, many Amboy people or any one of the players remember the game like it was yesterday. They speak fondly of one another and the value of teamwork and remember when the Perth Amboy basketball team was a champion.

Chapter 13

THE ARCHAEOLOGICAL DIG

1969–1976

From 1969 to 1976, Perth Amboy was the site of an archaeological dig supervised by Tony Massopust. Massopust is a biology teacher with an expertise in archaeology and a love for history. When not teaching biology at Perth Amboy High School, Massopust would spend his summers working for the State of New Jersey in archaeological digs from 1963 to 1968 in Warren County. "Massopust became interested in archeology when he participated in three summer digs for Indian artifacts with archeologists from New Jersey State Museum on the banks of the Delaware River in north Jersey. He later served as assistant field director for two summer Indian digs in the same locale sponsored by Seton Hall University."[100]

How did Tony Massopust get started with the dig? "That's a funny story," he states. Massopust is an Eagle Scout and had taken a group of Boy Scouts to the Sussex County dig at Miller's Field, where the workers were carefully digging up a bone.

"Why are you putting so much effort in digging up a deer bone?" Massopust asked the supervisor.

"Oh, you know bones? Want a job?" the supervisor asked Massopust.

"Yeah," Massopust answered.

"Okay," said the supervisor.

That is how Massopust got a job in the Indian dig. The following year, he was excavating at Miller's Field, and he would go on to work there for three years. The dig found early Woodland artifacts, including triangle points (projectile points or arrowheads). These items included such finds as Lenni-Lenape Indian bones and American Indian pottery and other artifacts. Massopust stated that the most interesting item found was a green chert (flint) drill made by a Lenape Indian for making holes in leather and wood. "It's now in the Trenton Museum," he proudly states.

Massopust enjoyed his experience in the Sussex and Warren County archaeological digs and decided to try excavating in Perth Amboy upon the suggestion of his wife, Marcella. She was inspired by her New York University American history of art professor, and she knew Tony had a background in archaeology. Tony was also inspired by Anna Cladek, the head librarian at the Perth Amboy Free Public Library, because she had a deep knowledge of Perth Amboy and knew a lot of people. "She was a very hard worker." Cladek saved all the terra cotta and the Women's Club Art Collection at the library.

The dig was funded by the Perth Amboy Recreation Department. "It didn't cost much—only about $4,000 to $5,000—and we reused the equipment the following years." Tony Massopust's cousin Frank Massopust made the screens the workers used, and the shovels came from the parks department. "We bought our own trowels."

The purpose of the archaeological project was to develop an interest in finding the historical artifacts in Perth Amboy. Massopust stated, "We took a dozen youths and we gave them something tangible to do for this city. I enjoyed watching the kids grow, and a lot of them still help the community and have a great interest in Perth Amboy."

The first dig was at Front and Smith Streets. It was sponsored by the Perth Amboy Recreation Department in coordination with Perth Amboy High School's summer program. The program began with the students first clearing the brushes away. Then, on July 8, 1969, the dig began. The area was divided in five- by five-foot blocks. The first three feet was discarded, and then they dug another five feet and sifted all the dirt to find what it contained. Many interesting items were found, including pipe stems dating from 1680–1720 (dates were estimated by the width of the pipes' diameters). Pieces of dishes and bowls from the colonial era were also discovered. They also found a cistern from the Civil War period that

The purpose of the archaeological project was to develop an interest in finding historical artifacts in Perth Amboy. Fred Taylor is at right. *Courtesy of the Massopust family.*

was used for water storage. "A lot of people didn't have running water back then, so they used cisterns." Inside the cistern, the workers found over one hundred intact bottles dating back to the 1890s and the bases of bottles dating back to 1685–1810. Massopust went on to find several cisterns and stated that was the most interesting discovery. The dig went on until August 14, 1969, when the holes were filled.

The second archaeological dig was in July and August 1970 and was located in Wisteria Place and Sadowski Parkway. The property was allowed to be excavated thanks to St. Demetrios Greek Orthodox Church. "We called it Calametrios," Massopust stated, "because we were between Caledonia Park and St. Demetrios." The students received no grades or credit for their work; it was purely for enrichment. They found many artifacts, including a sixteenth-century cannonball. The students

Tony Massopust said, "We took a dozen youths and we gave them something tangible to do for this city. I enjoyed watching the kids grow, and a lot of them still help the community and have a great interest in Perth Amboy." *Courtesy of the Massopust family.*

would come from 7:00 a.m. to 3:00 p.m., and Massopust would lecture them at 10:00 a.m. Often he had guest lecturers.

Massopust explains why the program is important: "It is to develop an interest in the history of Perth Amboy, to provide an opportunity for high school students to perform a tangible service to their community, to provide an activity for the youth of Perth Amboy who are interested in cultural and intellectual pursuits, and to find out about the Indian and Early Colonial period of city history, of which very little is known."[101]

Massopust felt that he learned that people do the same things in different periods of times in different ways. They all eat, procure food, dispose of waste and find places to sleep, and they do these things differently during different times. "It's a lot of periods—not just one—you have to look at the whole picture."

The next year, the dig was at the Ferry Slip, site of the famous Tottenville Ferry, which transported passengers from Perth Amboy to Staten Island and back. The following dig in the summer of 1972 was

Right: Many students enjoyed the summer learning about archaeology and the history of Perth Amboy. Nancy Telliho carries a box out of the Proprietary House. *Courtesy of the Massopust family.*

Below: Jim Lake (left) and Ralph Tabor (right) dig at the Proprietary House. *Courtesy of the Massopust family.*

at the Proprietary House at 149 Kearny Avenue. This dig lasted for three summers. Broken china and glassware were found, along with a late Woodland pendant. Funds to pay the students came from state and county grants. "We found a lot of nice artifacts."

All good things come to an end, and the final dig in the summer of 1976 was a program for special education students that took place off Mechanic Street. Little was found at this last dig, and Massopust went on to other projects.

Massopust felt that the archaeological digs got a lot of people interested in Perth Amboy and interested in history and archaeology, and they learned how to do a day's work. He was asked to speak at many historical societies and made a lot of contacts. He enjoyed his experiences at the Perth Amboy archaeological digs, and many students have fond memories of their summers digging for lost artifacts.

One student, Marianne Zanko, wrote a paper, "At the Dig," stating:

> *Sifters swiftly swing to and fro on their squeaky hinges as diggers scoop up piles of dirt, hurling them up and away into the hungry mouths of the screens...He cries out at the top of his lungs, "HEY MR. MASS! I'VE FOUND SOMETHING!"...Hearing the urgency of the cry, the red-bearded head archeologist, Anton J. Massopust, commences in haste to see the latest finding...Why do we do it? Because just as these proud colonial men and women kept going despite all opposition to capture the American Dream.*

Chapter 14

PERTH AMBOY CELEBRATES OUR NATION'S BICENTENNIAL

1973–1976

Anton J. Massopust was named chairman of the bicentennial by Perth Amboy's mayor, Alexander Jankowski. A committee was formed to undertake the task of organizing the events for the occasion. "The Committee will attempt to involve the city's public and private organization in the local celebration of our country's most important historical event,"[102] Massopust declared. Eleanor Bates chaired some of the events. During the bicentennial, many people, including Bates, Marion Kosh and Eleanor Dunay, sewed the costumes for the bicentennial events.

The bicentennial celebration was enjoyed by many throughout the city of Perth Amboy during 1975–76. In August 1975, art students painted fire hydrants in honor of the bicentennial. The hydrants were painted in the likeness of George Washington, Betsy Ross, General Casmir Pulaski and other historical figures. It was a joint effort by the bicentennial commission, the city fire department and the recreation department. Students put in five hours a day painting the fire hydrants. Massopust stated, "This is the first step in making the public aware of the activities planned by the commission."[103]

On Saturday, May 10, 1975, a crowd of fifteen thousand watched the Bicentennial Fireman's Heritage Parade. Over three thousand marchers and ninety fire trucks and ambulances commemorated the history of the

Anton Massopust II (my father) was chairman of the bicentennial from 1976 to 1977. Here he is dressed in a colonial costume. *Courtesy of the Massopust family.*

state's fire department. It was the kickoff for Perth Amboy's bicentennial celebration. Trucks dating back to 1917 were displayed. The three-mile route was filled with emergency apparatus. Antique cars were also in the parade. Awards were given for costumes and trucks during the celebration. First prize for best unit depicting firefighting then and now went to Cheesequake Fire Department. The best marching costume prize went to Wharton Fire Company. The best clown outfit went to Larry Deliman of the Perth Amboy Volunteer Fire Department. The best historic ambulance went to South Amboy First Aid Squad, and the most historic fire apparatus went to Madison Park Fire Department. The best women's auxiliary unit was South Amboy Ladies Auxiliary, and the best mascot was awarded to a Dalmatian owned by the Kingston Fire Department.

One hundred kegs of beer and ten thousand hot dogs were distributed at Mac William Stadium. Beer mugs were sold by various fire departments. There were bicentennial beer mugs on sale as well. If you bought a mug, you got a free beer and a hot dog. Two original oil paintings by local artist

Perth Amboy–born congressman Edward J. Patten speaks with Mayor Alexander F. Jankowski and others listening near the Proprietary House during the bicentennial. *Courtesy of Eleanor Bates.*

Francis McGinley were raffled off. A photographers' booth, where persons could be photographed next to an antique fire apparatus, was available to the public. Representative Edward J. Patten and Assemblyman George J. Otlowski attended the affair.

On Sunday, October 19, 1975, at 3:00 p.m., there was a nondenominational service, "Rededication to God: A Day of Repentance and Renewal." The service was supposed to take place at Bayview Park, but it rained. The service was therefore held at McGinnis School and was well attended. Every major church in Perth Amboy had clergy present.

January 3, 1976, at 8:00 p.m. featured the Bernardsville Pub Players in *Celebrate America: A Bicentennial Musical Revue*, which was performed at the Perth Amboy High School Auditorium. Act I featured regional melodies from New England, the Northeast, Midwest, South and West. Act II featured immigration, the Industrial Revolution, the era of conflicts and the era of progress. The show was enjoyed by many citizens.

From May 10 to 15, the Perth Amboy High School Bicentennial Cultural Arts Festival took place. It was held at Perth Amboy High School. There was music and singing.

On May 23 at 1:30 p.m., the Perth Amboy Bicentennial Commission, in conjunction with the Staten Island Historical Society, reenacted the peace talks that took place in the Conference House, home of Colonel Christopher Billopp, in Staten Island. In an attempt to avoid the Revolutionary War, Benjamin Franklin, John Adams and Edward Rutledge held the talks. When the talks broke down, Colonel Christopher Billopp was kidnapped and then returned to Perth Amboy, where the entire party was greeted with a fife and drum corps and Revolutionary War militia. The militia fired a 1,200-pound cannon in his honor. For the celebration, the kidnapping was reenacted, the actors rowed across the river to Staten Island and back and then, upon returning,

A battle between the Loyalists from Staten Island (Skinner's Greens) and the Continental Battery was reenacted for the bicentennial by an artillery group at the waterfront in Perth Amboy. *Courtesy of Eleanor Bates.*

the party was greeted by a fife and drum band and a militia that fired a 1,200-pound cannon.

On Saturday, June 5, 1976, at 1:30 p.m. and 5:00 p.m., the Hoxie Brothers Circus came to town. The circus grounds were between Front Street and High Street. The circus was in town for one day of fun and excitement for the whole family. They pitched their tent at 4:00 a.m. and left that night after the second performance. Advanced-sale tickets were $2.50 for adults and $1.50 for children under twelve. A small circus parade began at the high school and proceeded to the circus grounds. Massopust rode the elephant, as did Rose Chuback and Gerianne Bates, for the entire parade. The Perth Amboy High School Marching Band took part in the parade as well. Cleanup was fun for the local youths; they were given garbage bags and a dollar for every bag returned full of garbage.

On June 14, there was a raising of the bicentennial flag at City Hall Circle.

Chairman of the bicentennial Tony Massopust, Rose Chuback (a member of the bicentennial committee) and Gerianne Bates (on the little elephant) ride the elephants in the parade. *Courtesy of the Massopust family.*

Members of the bicentennial celebration pose for a photo. *Courtesy of Eleanor Bates.*

June 19 was the commemoration of the arrest of William Franklin at the Proprietary House at 149 Kearny Avenue. This was the first time the Proprietary House was opened up for visitors. The arrest of Franklin has been reenacted every year since, starring local entertainer Kurt Epps as William Franklin.

On Friday, July 2, at 8:30 p.m. at Perth Amboy High School, there was a presentation of the William Dunlap play *A Trip to Niagara*, directed by veteran actor Charlie White. It was followed by a candlelight reception at the high school. Admission was three dollars per person.

On Saturday, July 3, there was a huge bicentennial parade that began at City Hall Circle at 10:00 a.m. It featured a hand-knitted bicentennial flag made by Mrs. Terry Vona and carried by a group of women in colonial costumes. The parade also featured marching bands, floats and a costume competition. Later that day was the Bicentennial Country Fair, which was held at Water's Stadium. Featured were antique cars, crafts, competitions, games, food and fun for all. Admission was free.

On Saturday, July 3, 1976, there was a huge bicentennial parade that began in City Hall Circle at 10:00 a.m. It featured a hand-knitted bicentennial flag made by Mrs. Terry Vona and carried by a group of women in colonial costumes. *Left to right*: Debbie Orosky, Maryann Dunay, Christine Kosh, Nancy Bihary and Deborah Stephans. *Courtesy of Eleanor Bates.*

On Sunday, July 4, 1976, there was a memorial service at 10:00 a.m. at St. Peter's Episcopal Church on Rector Street. Conducting the service was Reverend Canon Russel Smith, ThD, Canon to the Ordinary and Archdeacon; Reverend Bailey Barnes; and Reverend J. Rodney Croes. The service was planned by the bicentennial committee and included a drum and fife band. Many of the congregation came in colonial costumes. The New Jersey Blues Revolutionary War reenactment group was present at the service, which was conducted from prayer books from colonial times. Honored was Reverend John Preston, rector of St. Peter's Episcopal Church until 1777. Reverend Preston was reverend and chaplain of the Twenty-sixth Regiment of England's soldiers quartered in Perth Amboy. He was loyal to England, while his congregation remained divided between the American

Patriots and England. Also honored was the Catholic involvement in the Revolutionary War. A pamphlet prepared by Reverend George Ahr, STD, was included in the program.

At 6:00 p.m., there was a bicentennial ball held at the Seven Arches. Tickets were eighteen dollars per person, and people were encouraged to come in colonial costumes. There an instructor demonstrated to guests how to perform many of the colonial dances, such as the minuet. Dinner included prime rib and an open bar.

On Monday, July 5, a band concert was held at Bayview Park at 3:00 p.m. by the Bay City Band. Admission was free.

During that year, there was a bicentennial poster contest. First prize went to Rosa Gonzales, and second prize went to Emily Kossowsky.

There was also a prize for the first bicentennial baby born in Perth Amboy. Rubin and Marta Delgado's son, Rubin Christopher Delgado, was presented with a certificate and a twenty-five-dollar savings bond by Massopust for being the first bicentennial baby born on July 4, 1976, at 6:32 p.m. at Raritan Bay Medical Center.

On Tuesday, August 24, the twenty-six-car American Freedom Train arrived in New Brunswick. Many people from Perth Amboy came into New Brunswick to see the famous Freedom Train. It was pulled by a 4-8-4 coal-burning steam engine. A 4-8-4 locomotive has four leading wheels, eight coupled driving wheels and four trailing wheels. It sometimes is referred to as a Northern. The train was built in 1945 and was a time capsule from the birth and growth of the United States. Visitors viewed the exhibits via a moving walkway. The concept of a moving walkway was devised by the Freedom Train Foundation planners to allow as many people as possible to see the display. The walkway took people through ten exhibit cars that show American life from colonial to present time. Memorabilia from Presidents Abraham Lincoln, Franklin D. Roosevelt and John F. Kennedy were on display. Replicas of the Declaration of Independence and other documents were on the train. There was even featured Dorothy's ruby slippers from the MGM classic movie *The Wizard of Oz*. Armed guards watched over the memorabilia. The train began its journey on April 1, 1975, and ended in December 1976 in Miami.

Massopust was honored for his work as bicentennial chairman with a plaque stating:

PRESENTED TO
ANTON MASSOPUST
CHAIRMAN
PERTH AMBOY BICENTENNIAL COMMISSION
FOR OUTSTANDING KNOWLEDGE OF
THE RICH HISTORY
OF
THE CITY OF PERTH AMBOY
STATE OF NEW JERSEY
JULY 4, 1976

Chapter 15

CELEBRATE PERTH AMBOY

The Bill of Rights Bicentennial Celebration
November 20, 1989

In 1789, Perth Amboy was the state capital and was the site of legislative sessions, including the session that first ratified the Bill of Rights. Today, it holds the distinction of having the oldest functioning city hall in the United States.

Celebrate Perth Amboy sponsored the four-day extravaganza starting on Thursday, November 16, 1989, recognizing the city as the site of the first ratification of the Bill of Rights. Barry Rosengarten was chairman of the Celebrate Perth Amboy Committee. The celebration began with one hundred people being sworn in to citizenship on Friday, November 17, 1989, in City Hall Circle. A colonial fair was held on Saturday, November 18, in City Hall Circle, where the newly built Bill of Rights arch stands and was dedicated in front of city hall. This arch is a historically accurate replica of one of the city's original arches that stood welcoming people to shop in Market Square. Commemorative bricks in the arch were sold to citizens for one dollar apiece to commemorate Market Square. Anyone who purchased a brick received a certificate with his or her name on it and a paperweight with the "Celebrate Perth Amboy" logo on it. A pendant was offered for a twenty-five-dollar donation.

There was a parade down Market Street to City Hall Circle with an army band from Fort Dix, and a student band also performed. A guided

Celebrate Perth Amboy

Barry Rosengarten chaired Celebrate Perth Amboy, and these bumper stickers were put out to commemorate the event. *Courtesy of the Massopust family.*

missile destroyer, the USS *Lawrence*, was docked in Perth Amboy harbor for the celebration and was open for tours.

During the 1980s, more than half the residents of Perth Amboy were Puerto Rican; therefore, the Puerto Rican flag was raised in City Hall Circle to honor the city's citizens. An interfaith service was held at Temple Beth Mordecai on High Street to celebrate the diverse religious backgrounds in Perth Amboy.

A black-tie affair at the Armory Restaurant was held by the Proprietary House Historical Society on Sunday, November 19. The event featured New Jersey's authentic copy of the Bill of Rights on display at the Armory.

A special legislative session was held at 10:30 a.m. on Monday, November 20, 1989, at McGinnis School on State Street to commemorate the act, with those present including Governor Thomas H. Kean, Senator Frank R. Lautenberg and Ronald L. Trowbridge, head of staff for the Commission on the Bicentennial of the U.S. Constitution. Senator Frank R. Lautenberg stated that the Bill of Rights is "a living document."

This ceremony was followed with a costumed reenactment of the Bill of Rights ratification in City Hall Circle, several feet from where the actual ratification took place on November 20, 1789. Benjamin Franklin was portrayed by veteran actor Charlie White of Perth Amboy, who led a discussion on the importance of the Bill of Rights and how Benjamin Franklin fought for civil rights until the day he died. Anton J. Massopust III portrayed Benjamin Franklin's grandson (son of Royal Governor William Franklin), William Temple Franklin. Other Perth Amboy citizens represented each amendment in the Bill of Rights and their importance. At the end, they shouted out each amendment in the Bill of Rights, declaring liberty. The celebration was filmed for Perth Amboy

Above: The Spirit of '76, a trio of musicians who appeared at reenactment events. They appeared in Perth Amboy at the Bill of Rights reenactment on November 20, 1989, in City Hall Circle. *Courtesy of the Massopust family.*

Left: Anton Massopust III portrayed William Temple Franklin and local actor Charlie White portrayed Benjamin Franklin in the ceremonies. *Courtesy of the Massopust family.*

On November 20, 1789, the Bill of Rights was signed in Perth Amboy. Reenacting the event on November 20, 1989, were Tony Massopust, John K. Dyke, Kurt Epps and J.V. Costello. *Courtesy of the Massopust family.*

These reenactors pose at Celebrate Perth Amboy in City Hall Circle. *Courtesy of the Massopust family.*

television and ABC *Eyewitness News*. A commercial was filmed advertising the market fair that was aired on PA-TV. Thousands came to City Hall Circle to watch the reenactment.

A commemorative rubber-stamp cancellation by the U.S. Post Office was issued declaring, "We signed it first!" Two custom-made "We signed it first!" stampers were approved for Perth Amboy to be used on Monday, November 20, 1989. They had to be returned to the U.S. government thirty days later. A Bill of Rights stamp was also issued to commemorate the event, along with an official envelope.

Chapter 16

PERTH AMBOY HONORS ITS VETERANS WITH A MILITARY TIMELINE MURAL IN THE CITY COUNCIL CHAMBERS

June 2009–November 2009

Mayor Wilda Diaz wished to honor the veterans of Perth Amboy by having a permanent mural painted and dedicated to the brave men and women from Perth Amboy who have served or who are serving in the armed forces. It is important to understand that many people from Perth Amboy throughout the years have dedicated their service and lives for our country's freedom. The mural represents a military timeline depicting the armed forces from colonial times to the present. The mural was painted by the Perth Amboy High School Gifted and Talented Art students under the supervision of Mrs. Marcella Massopust.

Marcella Massopust was asked to paint the mural with her Gifted and Talented students in the spring of 2009 and began painting during the summer of 2009. Massopust had been teaching art for over forty years, and for the past twenty-five years, Mrs. Massopust's many students have painted Christmas murals in the hospital boiler room window, which have been a welcome sight for people driving by Raritan Bay Medical Center. The Gifted and Talented students have also painted a permanent mural in Raritan Bay Medical Center's maternity ward and a multitude of permanent historical murals in Perth Amboy High School. In early 2009, the students completed a mural on the history of theater throughout the ages located near the Perth Amboy High School auditorium.

The students involved in the mural project were Julisa Mugica (eighteen), Sadie Viscainio (eighteen), Wilson Inoa Tejada (seventeen), Tito Mantilla (seventeen), Mehgan Reyes (sixteen) and Yesenia Feliciano (seventeen). Mugica and Viscainio both started college during the fall of 2009 and majored in art. Former Perth Amboy High School Gifted and Talented art student Maria Elena Grande did the lettering.

The Gifted and Talented Art Program at Perth Amboy High School offers a conceptual approach to learning art through solving artistic problems. It emphasizes creativity and the students' ability to think for themselves. Art appreciation is included in the program. The Gifted and Talented Art curriculum offers college credit through the AP program and through acceptance in the Middlesex County Arts High School.

Sadie Viscainio begins painting the mural in the city hall council chambers. *Photo by the author.*

Original plaques with names of veterans of past wars are preserved and displayed already in the chambers. A military timeline is portrayed through a series of paintings of military personnel from the Revolutionary War to the present day. Assistant city historian Anton J. Massopust advised on the historical accuracy of the military uniforms.

Prominent citizens who served our country include William Dunlap's father, Samuel, who served with General Wolfe's regiment during the French and Indian War. During the period of the long conflict with France and its Indian allies, the royal governor of New Jersey, William Franklin, served in the local militia, reaching the rank of captain. The people of Perth Amboy fought in the War for Independence, unfortunately on both sides. The bullet holes in the tombstones in St. Peter's Cemetery give evidence of this struggle. Perth Amboy men fought in the Civil War with the New Jersey Brigade, which fought from the First Battle of Bull Run to the surrender at Appomattox. Commodore Lawrence Kearny, known as "the sailor diplomat," was the first person to open up trade with China.

The Perth Amboy High School Gifted and Talented class continues to paint the mural. *Photo by the author.*

He commanded the frigate *Constellation* and was known for his efforts in fighting Greek pirates in the Mediterranean Sea.

Michael J. Krochmally Jr. was the first Perth Amboyan to give his life in World War I.

During World War II, Perth Amboy did its part. There are many reminders in town. Just take a look around Perth Amboy to see the many streets and parks that serve as reminders to those who have bravely served and gave their lives for our country. The first Perth Amboy citizen to give his life in World War II was Neal Lucey, for whom the Lucey Center is named. He was on the USS *Arizona* when Pearl Harbor was attacked. Arneson Square is dedicated to Robert Arneson, who died of his wounds received at Pearl Harbor. Steve "Spike" Kosymyna was the most decorated soldier from World War II from Perth Amboy. Rudyk Park is in memory of Stanley Rudyk, who was killed in Tunisia. Sergeant Joseph J. Sadowski received the Congressional Medal of Honor posthumously for his action in the European theater. Perth Amboy's beautiful waterfront drive is named in memory of him. John Petach flew with the RAF in the Flying Tigers. In 1942, he volunteered for an extra two weeks of deployment and was killed in action. The film and book *God Is My Co-Pilot* depicts his courageous spirit.

Many Perth Amboy citizens served in the Korean War, Vietnam and Desert Storm. Presently, many citizens serve in Iraq or Afghanistan.

Many people will see the plaques on the walls in the chambers, or those who walk along Sadowski Parkway will see the veterans' memorial, dedicated on May 30, 2005. The memorial contains the names of everyone from Perth Amboy who served in the military. The names on the walls tell many stories of families from our city. Every name represents a family of a veteran who served his or her country.

Benjamin Franklin said, "There is no such thing as a good war or a bad peace." No matter what the cause, Perth Amboy responded to do its part. It may have been tedious labor or dangerous assignments, but Perth Amboy's men were there. In the Civil War, James Kearny Smith served from the First Battle of Bull Run until he was wounded for the third time at Fredericksburg, was captured and became a prisoner of war until the end of the war. Little is known of him except that he, like thousands of Perth Amboy citizens, gave a large part of his life to serve his country. If asked, it is certain that they would all do it again.

The Gifted and Talented class is almost finished with the mural. *Photo by the author.*

Dedicated in 2005, the War Memorial contains the names of all from Perth Amboy who have served in the armed forces. *Photo by the author.*

The mural is seen by all who come to a meeting or visit our city council chambers. They see the names on the wall and the mural, and it is hoped that they will remind them of our military history. May they remember all the men and women from Perth Amboy who wore the uniforms for our country. Always remember we are the Land of the Free because of the Brave.

The mural was formally unveiled on Veterans Day, November 11, 2009. Perth Amboy's veterans pulled the string while being hailed by the Middlesex County Police and Fire Piper and Drum Corps. Many citizens watched the dedication in city hall chambers. Marcella Massopust and her students all received citations from Mayor Wilda Diaz for their work.

This mural was the first of many memorials Perth Amboy dedicated under Mayor Diaz. In 2011, the Fallen Officers Memorial, the 9-11 Memorial and the Purple Heart Monument were all dedicated.

The Fallen Officers Memorial was dedicated on June 22, 2011, at a ceremony that was held inside the YMCA Complex in front of the

The Middlesex County Police and Fire Piper and Drum Corps played at the unveiling of the mural on November 11, 2009. *Photo by the author.*

Above: The Gifted and Talented class with Mayor Wilda Diaz and Marcella Massopust. *Left to right*: Mayor Wilda Diaz, Tito Mantilla, Mehgan Reyes, Yesenia Feliciano, Sadie Viscainio, Julisa Mugica, Wilson Inoa Tejada and Gifted and Talented art teacher Marcella Massopust. *Photo by the author.*

Right: The Fallen Officers Memorial. The statue portrays St. Michael, patron saint of police officers. *Photo by Paul W. Wang.*

courthouse. A large crowd in attendance, including police officers, city officials, citizens and clergy, stood under threatening weather to witness the unveiling of the memorial. The memorial is dedicated to Thomas E. Raji, the first police officer from Perth Amboy to die in the line of duty, who died on August 22, 2008. The statue portrays St. Michael, patron saint of police officers, protecting an officer in the likeness of Raji and his dog.

In 2011, it was the tenth anniversary of the tragedy of 9-11. Getting support to put in a proper base for a 9-11 Memorial on Sadowski Parkway was easy for local artist Tom Ward. For years, Police Officer Harry Scheman had been holding a candlelit service at Market Square on the anniversary of 9-11. Scheman jumped at the chance to create a permanent memorial at the site, especially with the tenth anniversary in 2011. Ward got in touch with Guy Hogan, who has made his mark as a visionary with his efforts to restore the Proprietary House. After that, there never was a time when these two were not planning, designing and gathering support for the project. The 9-11 Memorial was dedicated to Perth Amboy residents Isaias Rivera and Richard Rodriguez, who lost

The 9-11 Memorial is located in City Hall Circle. *Photo by Paul W. Wang.*

The 9-11 Memorial was dedicated to Perth Amboy residents Isaias Rivera and Richard Rodriguez, who lost their lives at the World Trade Center on 9-11. The memorial was dedicated on the tenth anniversary of 9-11. *Photo by Paul W. Wang.*

Anthony Yelensics Chapter 181 dedicated the Purple Heart Monument located at the waterfront on Sadowski Parkway across from St. Demetrios Church. *Photo by Paul W. Wang.*

The Purple Heart Monument was dedicated on October 15, 2011. Chapter Commander Walter P. Kaczmarek, Mayor Diaz and State Commander Neil Vaness made remarks. This was the fourth dedication of a Purple Heart monument in New Jersey. *Photo by Paul W. Wang*

their lives at the World Trade Center on 9-11. Several local contractors volunteered their labor to see to it that the project was completed on time. The memorial was dedicated on the tenth anniversary of 9-11. All who supported the project received citations or proclamations from the mayor.

Anthony Yelensics Chapter 181 dedicated the Purple Heart Monument located at the waterfront on Sadowski Parkway across from St. Demetrios Church. This was the fourth dedication of a Purple Heart monument in New Jersey. Chapter commander Walter P. Kaczmarek, Mayor Diaz and State Commander Neil Vaness made remarks. The Purple Heart Monument was dedicated on October 15, 2011.

AFTERWORD

These special moments live in the hearts of the individuals and the lives that they touched. Today, more moments in history are created each day. The future of Perth Amboy holds more stories to tell of this historic and unique city.

Notes

Introduction

1. Whitehead, *Early History of Perth Amboy*, 5.

Chapter 1

2. Skemp, *William Franklin*, 4.
3. Isaacson, *Benjamin Franklin*, 76.
4. Skemp, *William Franklin*, 4–5.
5. Ibid., xii.
6. *Franklin's Writings*, Vol. VII, 158.
7. Morgan, *Benjamin Franklin*, 240.
8. Randall, *A Little Revenge*, 182.
9. Whitehead, *History of Perth Amboy, N.J.*, 191.
10. Ibid.
11. Randall, *A Little Revenge*, 243.
12. Ibid., 192.
13. Ibid., 243.
14. Dudas, "History of Perth Amboy."

15. Randall, *A Little Revenge*, 256.

16. Mariobe, *Life of Franklin*, vol. 1, 130.

17. William Franklin to Lord Dartmouth, January 8, 1776, 699–700, as quoted in Skemp, *William Franklin*, 194.

18. William Franklin to William Winds, January 9, 1776, Duer Stirling, 120–21, as quoted in Skemp, *William Franklin*, 195.

19. William Franklin to Lord Germain, March 28, 1776, F.W. Ricord, ed., *Documents Relating to the Colonial History of the State of New Jersey*, 10:705–6, as quoted in Skemp, *William Franklin*, 197.

20. Minutes of the Provincial Council of Safety of the State of New Jersey, 456.

21. Randall, *A Little Revenge*, 496.

CHAPTER 2

22. Mills, *Historic Houses of New Jersey*, 141.

23. Ibid., 142.

24. Ibid., 142–43.

25. Ibid., 141.

26. Ibid.

27. Ibid., 143.

28. Ibid., 147.

29. Ibid., 148–49.

30. Ibid., 150.

CHAPTER 3

31. Isenberg, *Fallen Founder*, vii.

32. Ibid., 11.

33. Ibid., 77.

34. Ibid., 179–80.

35. Ibid., 186.

36. Ibid., 196.

37. Fleming, *Duel*, 100.

38. Ibid.

39. Ibid., 101.
40. Ibid., 265.
41. Ibid., 287–88.

CHAPTER 4

42. Alden, *Lawrence Kearny*, 14.
43. Ibid., 39.
44. Ibid., v–vi.
45. Ibid., 222–23.

CHAPTER 5

46. Whitman, "He Flew an Airship," 15.
47. Andrenz, *Genealogical History*, 264.
48. Miers, *Where the Raritan Flows*, 72.
49. Whitman, "He Flew an Airship," 18.
50. Miers, *Where the Raritan Flows*, 77–78.
51. Ibid., 78.
52. Whitman, "He Flew an Airship," 18.
53. Ibid., 123.
54. Ibid., 123–24.
55. Ibid., 124.
56. Ibid.
57. Ibid.
58. Ibid.
59. Ibid., 125.
60. "Count Ferdinand von Zeppelin," www.airships.net/count-ferdinand-von-zeppelin.

CHAPTER 6

61. Mullaney, "Feminism, Utopianism, and Domesticity," 5.
62. Ibid., 6.
63. Ibid., 5.

64. Barkin, "Rebecca Buffum Spring."
65. Warren, "Uncle Marcus," 18.
66. Ibid., 17.
67. Ibid., 20.
68. Ibid., 16–17.
69. "Provisional Prospectus of the Raritan Bay Union."
70. Ibid.
71. Boyler, "Last of Eagleswood."
72. Warren, "Uncle Marcus," 17–18.
73. Rebecca Spring, "A Book of Remembrance," 109–10, as quoted in Barkin, "Rebecca Buffum Spring."
74. Rebecca Spring, "A Book of Remembrance," 110–11, as quoted in Barkin, "Rebecca Buffum Spring."
75. *News Tribune*, "Raritan Bay Union's Eagleswood."
76. *Perth Amboy Evening News*, "Eagleswood Dream a Failure."
77. Cagney, "Eagleswood."
78. Mullaney, "Feminism, Utopianism, and Domesticity," 6.

CHAPTER 7

79. McGinnis, *History of Perth Amboy*, 139.
80. Ibid.

CHAPTER 8

81. *New York Times*, "7 Firemen Killed."
82. Ibid.
83. Ibid.
84. *Perth Amboy Evening News*, "6 Firemen Killed."
85. *New York Times*, "7 Firemen Killed."
86. Massopust, *History of the Perth Amboy Fire Department*.
87. *Perth Amboy Evening News*, "6 Firemen Killed."

Chapter 9

88. Furer, "Perth Amboy Riots," 211.

89. *New York Times*.

90. This is documented in a PBS interview with Edward J. Patten, circa 1980 (mayor of Perth Amboy, 1934–40; House of Representatives Fifteenth District, 1963–80), who was also a participant in the riot.

91. *Perth Amboy Evening News*, "City Quiet After Night Riot."

92. Ibid.

93. Gentry, "Mayor Unaware of Big Riot."

94. Furer, "Perth Amboy Riots," 229.

Chapter 10

95. "America on Wheels: Largest Chain of Roller Skating Rinks on East Coast." www.usarsarollerskaters.org/americaonwheels.html.

Chapter 11

96. Malwitz, "Remembering the Explosion."

Chapter 12

97. *Perth Amboy Evening News*, "Perth Amboy Has Never Won Big Title."

98. Konick, "Perth Amboy in Finals."

99. *Perth Amboy Evening News*, "Taylor's Heroics."

Chapter 13

100. *Sunday Home News*, "Teens Take Backward Step."

101. Geissler, "Museum for City Suggested."

Chapter 14

102. *News Tribune*, "City Names Massopust."

103. *News Tribune*, "Hydrants Join Bicentennial."

BIBLIOGRAPHY

INTRODUCTION

Whitehead, William A. Early History of Perth Amboy and Adjoining Country with Sketches of Men and Events in New Jersey During the Provincial Era. New York: D. Appleton & Company, 1856.

CHAPTER 1

Dudas, Jack M. "A History of Perth Amboy 1683–1983." *Perth Amboy Tercentennial*, June 13, 1983.

Isaacson, Walter. *Benjamin Franklin: An American Life*. New York: Simon & Schuster, 2003.

Mariobe, William Herbert. *The Life of Franklin*. Ann Arbor, MI: University Microfilms, 1962.

Minutes of the Provincial Council of Safety of the State of New Jersey.

Morgan, Edmund S. *Benjamin Franklin*. Chicago: R.R. Donnelley & Sons, 2002.

Randall, Willard Sterne. *A Little Revenge: Benjamin Franklin and His Son*. Boston: Little Brown and Company, 1984.

Skemp, Shelia L. *William Franklin: Son of a Patriot, Servant of a King*. New York: Oxford University Press, 1990.

Smyth, Albert Henry, *The Writings of Benjamin Franklin Vol. VII, 1777–1779*. New York: Macmillan Press, 1906.

Whitehead, William A. *History of Perth Amboy and Adjoining Country with Sketches of Men and Events in New Jersey During the Provincial Era*. New York: D. Appleton & Company, 1856.

CHAPTER 2

Alden, Carroll Storrs. *Lawrence Kearny: Sailor Diplomat*. Princeton, NJ: Princeton University Press, 1936.

Gleaves, Albert. *James Lawrence, Captain United States Navy: Commander of the Chesapeake*. New York: J.B. Putnam's Sons, 1904.

Mills, W.J. *Historic Houses of New Jersey*. Philadelphia: J.B. Lippincott Co., 1902.

"Richard Lawrence, U.E. of New Jersey." RootsWeb. wc.rootsweb. ancestry.com/cgi-bin/igm.cgi?op=GET&db=all2getherl&id=I369.

CHAPTER 3

"Aaron Burr." Knowledgerush. www.knowledgerush.com/kr/ encyclopedia/Aaron_Burr.

Fleming, Thomas. *Duel: Alexander Hamilton, Aaron Burr and the Future of America*. New York: Basic Books, 1999.

Isenberg, Nancy. *Fallen Founder: The Life of Aaron Burr*. New York: Penguin Group, 2007.

Pickersgill, Harold E. *The Exchange Club of Perth Amboy, Nova Caesaria and Ompoge Point Which Later Became New Jersey and Perth Amboy*. Perth Amboy, NJ: Pickersgill Press, 1937, 32–33.

CHAPTER 4

Alden, Carroll Storrs. *Lawrence Kearny: Sailor Diplomat*. Princeton, NJ: Princeton University Press, 1936.

"Commodore Lawrence Kearny." mysite.verizon.net/sepulcher/Commodore.html.

Pickersgill, Harold E. *The Exchange Club of Perth Amboy, Nova Caesaria and Ompoge Point Which Later Became New Jersey and Perth Amboy*. Perth Amboy: Pickersgill Press, 1937, 45–46.

CHAPTER 5

Andrenz, Alfred. *Genealogical History of John and Mary Andrews Who Settled in Farmington*. Chicago: A.H. Andrews & Co., 1872.

"Count Ferdinand von Zeppelin." Airships: The Hindenburg and Other Zeppelins. www.airships.net/count-ferdinand-von-zeppelin.

Miers, Earl Shenck. *Where the Raritan Flows*. New Brunswick, NJ: Rutgers University Press, 1964, 71–87.

Pickersgill, Harold E. *The Exchange Club of Perth Amboy, Nova Caesaria and Ompoge Point Which Later Became New Jersey and Perth Amboy*. Perth Amboy, NJ: Pickersgill Press, 1937, 40–43.

"Solomon Andrews." 1992 Pioneer Inductees. www.njinvent.org/1992/pioneer_inductees_1992/andrews.html.

"Solomon Andrews, MD." www.kinnexions.com/kinnexions/cousinsa.htm.

Whitman, Roger B. "He Flew an Airship Before the Wrights Were Born!" *Popular Science Monthly*, January 1932.

CHAPTER 6

Barkin, Sarah. "Rebecca Buffum Spring and the Politics of Motherhood in Antebellum America." Presented at the Susan B. Anthony conference held at the University of Rochester, Rochester, NY, March 2006. hdl.handle.net/1802/2471.

Boyler, Gary. "The Last of Eagleswood ." *News Tribune*, August 22, 1975.

Cagney, Frances. "Eagleswood: A Local Social Experiment Attracted Literary Giants of the 1800s." *Perth Amboy Evening News*, November 12, 1949.

Middlesex County Democrat. "Death of Marcus Spring." August 22, 1874.

Mullaney, Marie Marmo. "Feminism, Utopianism, and Domesticity: The Career of Rebecca Buffum Spring, 1811–1911." *New Jersey History* 104, no. 3–4 (1987).

News Tribune. "Raritan Bay Union's Eagleswood of Mid-1800s Claimed Education As Its Principle Objective." N.d.

Perera, Eve Lewis, and Lucille Salitan, eds. "A Visit to John Brown." In *Virtuous Lives: Four Quaker Sisters Remember Family Life, Abolitionism and Women's Suffrage.* New York: Continuum, 1994.

Perth Amboy Evening News. "Eagleswood Dream a Failure." June 22, 1959.

———. "Eagleswood Sought Utopia." September 19, 1953.

———. "Woman Who Died Here This Week Knew Civil War Abolitionist Well." March 13, 1942.

"Provisional Prospectus of the Raritan Bay Union."

Warren, Dale. "Uncle Marcus." *New-England Galaxy* 9, no. 1 (Summer 1967): 16–26.

CHAPTER 7

McGinnis, William C. *History of Perth Amboy (1651–1959).* Vol. II. Perth Amboy, NJ: American Pub. Co., 1959.

Perth Amboy Evening News. "First Negro Voter." June 22, 1959.

———. "Local Church to Honor Voter Who Made History." October 31, 1959.

———. "Medal Awarded to Local Negro Bought by University in Louisiana." February 19, 1948.

———. "Mundy Exercised His Right." December 5, 1977.

Pickersgill, Harold E. *The Exchange Club of Perth Amboy, Nova Caesaria and Ompoge Point Which Later Became New Jersey and Perth Amboy.* Perth Amboy, NJ: Pickersgill Press, 1937, 30–32.

Sullivan, Gary. "His Vote Made All the Difference." *News Tribune,* December 5, 1977.

CHAPTER 8

Massopust, Lt. Anton J. *The History of the Perth Amboy Fire Department*. Perth Amboy, NJ, 2006.

New York Times. "7 Firemen Killed As Truck Hits Train; Safety Gate Open." June 16, 1921.

Perth Amboy Evening News. "Crossing Crash Death Toll Grows to 9 As 3 More Firemen Die in Hospital: Probes Are Under Way." June 16, 1921.

———. "Pray at Eagle Fire House for Recovery of Victims." June 16, 1921.

———. "6 Firemen Killed in Crash with Express Train at Market St. Crossing; Many Hurt." June 15, 1921.

———. "Two Investigations Started to Fix the Responsibility." June 16, 1921.

CHAPTER 9

Furer, Howard B. "The Perth Amboy Riots of 1923." *New Jersey History* 87 (1969): 211–25.

Gentry, Earl. "Mayor Unaware of Big Riot Last Night." *Perth Amboy Evening News*, August 31, 1923.

New York Times, June 6, 1923.

PBS interview with Edward J. Patten, circa 1980.

Perth Amboy Evening News. "City Quiet after Night Riot: Second Attempt to Organize Klan Frustrated by Mob Which Stormed Odd Fellows Hall Here Last Night." August 31, 1923.

CHAPTER 10

"America on Wheels: Largest Chain of Roller Skating Rinks on East Coast." www.usarsarollerskaters.org/americaonwheels.html.

"History of Roller Skating." Skatingfitness.com. www.skatingfitness.com/RollerSkating-History-of-Roller-Skating.htm.

CHAPTER 11

Malwitz, Rick. "Remembering the Explosion that Rocked South Amboy 60 Years Ago." MyCentralJersey.com, May 15, 2010.

CHAPTER 12

Goldberg, David. "Big 3—Cason, Somogyi, Taylor." *Perth Amboy Evening News*, April 3, 1968.

Konick, Emery, Jr. "Amboy Accents Team Play." *Perth Amboy Evening News*, March 18, 1968.

———. "Amboy Advances in Semis." *Perth Amboy Evening News*, March 13, 1968.

———. "Amboy's Taylor Adjusting Sights." *Perth Amboy Evening News*, January 24, 1968.

———. "Konick's Corner." *Perth Amboy Evening News*, April 4, 1968.

———. "Perth Amboy in Finals." *Perth Amboy Evening News*, March 25, 1968.

———. "Perth Amboy Is Number 1." *Perth Amboy Evening News*, April 1, 1968.

———. "Taylor Powers Panthers." *Perth Amboy Evening News*, March 25, 1968.

News Tribune. "Brian Taylor Mulling Seven Bonafide Offers." September 15, 1978.

Perth Amboy Evening News. "Amboy Must Scuttle Hackensack Slowdown." March 22, 1968.

———. "Amboy Tops on Offense." January 19, 1968.

———. "Famine Ends." March 25, 1968.

———. "Perth Amboy Has Never Won Big Title." March 30, 1968.

———. "Spotlight on Perth." March 11, 1968.

———. "Taylor's Heroics Give Amboy State Crown." April 1, 1968.

CHAPTER 13

Atom Tabloid. "Massopust Reports on Archeological Dig." February 5, 1975.

Esposito, Frank J. "Your Central Jersey: Traveler's Notebook—No. 58." *Sunday Home News*, July 23, 1972.

Ferencsik, Dianne. "Funds Set for Youth Program." *News Tribune*, August 5, 1976.

Geissler, Judy. "Museum for City Suggested." *News Tribune*, September 3, 1970.

Heller, Richard. "Young Archeologists Seldom Get Bored." *News Tribune*, August 17, 1971.

Levy, Amy. "City Teens Dig Summer in Project." *News Tribune*, September 6, 1969.

Molnar, Alan. "Youths Dig for Artifacts." *News Tribune*, July 23, 1975.

Savage, Ana. "A Perth Amboy Teacher Seeks to Trace and Preserve a Mansion's Heritage." *New York Times*, August 12, 1973.

Stek, Vera C. "Relics Unearthed in City." *News Tribune*, January 12, 1976.

Sunday Home News. "Teens Take Backward Step, Learn a Lot." August 13, 1972.

CHAPTER 14

Fischer, John J. "Train Exhibit Carries Birth, Growth of U.S." *News Tribune*, August 25, 1976.

Lanman, Sandra. "Perth Amboy Marchers Kick Off Bicentennial." *Home News*, May 12, 1975.

News Tribune. "Bicentennial Launched in Perth Amboy." May 12, 1975.

———. "City Names Massopust to Form Bicentennial Plans." March 7, 1973.

———. "Hydrants Join Bicentennial." August 22, 1975.

CHAPTER 15

Beckerman, Jim. "Stamp Put on History." *News Tribune*, November 21, 1989.

Cotter, Kelly-Jane. "'Celebrate Perth Amboy' Begins: City's Bill of Rights Ratification Basis for Four Days of Festivities." *Home News*, November 16, 1989.

Haydon, Tom. "Bill of Rights 'Ratified' Anew to Mark 200th." *News Tribune*, November 21, 1989.

Kuhn, Michele J. "A Place in History: Perth Amboy Puts Mark on Bill of Rights—Again." *News Tribune*, November 21, 1989.

Quigley, Mary Alice. "New Jersey's Ratification of the Bill of Rights." *New Jersey Historical Commission Newsletter* 20, no. 3 (November 1989).

Yourstone, Wayne F. "Joy for Newest Americans." *News Tribune*, November 19, 1989.

About the Author

Katherine Massopust earned a bachelor's degree in physics and mathematics from Muhlenberg College in Allentown, Pennsylvania, in 1989 and a master's degree in applied physics from Appalachian State University in Boone, North Carolina, in 1992. Katherine's articles have been featured in the *Amboy Beacon*, a local newspaper that served the Perth Amboy community for years. Presently she is a staff writer and the layout coordinator for the *Amboy Guardian*,  the present local newspaper. Katherine is the coauthor along with her husband, Paul W. Wang, of Arcadia Publishing's *Then & Now: Perth Amboy*.

Katherine Massopust is an active member of the Kearny Cottage Historical Society, a local society dedicated to preserving the home of Commodore Lawrence Kearny. She served as recording secretary for the society for six years and is presently a trustee. Katherine is also the founding president of the Friends of Perth Amboy Free Public Library. She also is serving as a member of the Historic Preservation Commission. Katherine enjoys playing softball and swimming, embroidering and watching baseball in her free time.

Visit us at
www.historypress.net